ACHIEVING BE
GOL

PRACTICAL HANDBOOK

ACHIEVING BETTER GOLF

STEVE NEWELL AND PAUL FOSTON

This Paperback edition published by
Hermes House an imprint of
Aneess Publishing Limited
Hermes House 88-89 Blackfriars Road,
London SE1 8HA

A CIP catalogue record for this book is available from the British Library

ISBN 1 84038 802 1

Publisher: Joanna Lorenz
Senior Editor: Belinda Wilkinson
Project Editor: Graham Smith
Photographer: David Cannon
Illustrator: Michael Shoebridge
Production Controller: Don Campaniello

Also published as *How to Play Golf*

Printed and bound in Hong Kong

10 9 8 7 6 5 4 3 2 1

CONTENTS

INTRODUCTION

Golf is probably the most fascinating, enjoyable, addictive and yet frustratingly irritating game you can ever take up. A game where you can hit a perfect drive and a perfect pitch on to the green . . . and then take three putts to hole from five feet. A game where you can play the round of your dreams one day . . . and a round from your worst nightmares the next. And yet . . . there are the glorious days when everything slides into place. Days when every shot is accompanied by the click of golf ball on sweet spot. Days when the hole really does seem as large as the proverbial bucket, and every drive soars like an eagle. These are the days that send golfers flocking back to the course for more.

This book can help bring you closer to your vision of golfing happiness. Whether you are a complete beginner or have years of experience, you will find something here to help you. If you are new to the game, you will appreciate the clear explanations of basic technique, and the pointers which will help you develop your skill and ability. For more advanced players, there are tips on shaping your shots, coping with hazards and obstacles, and on course strategy. And players at all levels can benefit from the troubleshooting hints and the practice drills which can help you refine your game to its full potential.

It is easy to get hooked on the golfing drug. But unlike a drug that promises short-lived, artificial highs, good golf instruction offers the very real prospect of longer-lasting, more euphoric after-effects - namely lower scores and a lifetime's addiction to the game. So let's see how you do.

Steve Newell

RAY COOK
RAY COOK
RAY COOK
RAY COOK

CHAPTER 1

Choosing the tools of any trade should never be taken lightly. And for the time being, you can forget the old saying about a workman not blaming his tools. With golf, the equipment you use can make a difference. So, given the complexities of swinging a small clubhead several feet at speeds of up to 120mph with the intention of making contact with a smallish ball, you'd better make sure your golf equipment is helping, not hindering you.

EQUIPMENT

THE TOOLS OF THE TRADE

● Choosing a club from the array of designs on offer can be a bewildering experience, as each new development promises to transform your game. If you are a beginner, you might be advised to purchase second-hand, as a well-cared-for set of good-quality used clubs is often a better bet than a new set of cheaper manufacture. It is also worthwhile to take advice from a good coach or the club professional before parting with hard-earned cash. In the end though, only you can decide what feels right for your shape, strength and style of play.

JOIN THE CLUB

Each club has subtly different characteristics. Irons are numbered from 2 to 9, with a 2-iron having its face angled at 18° from the vertical. This loft angle is increased by 4° for each higher numbered iron. The shaft also reduces in length as the club number increases, demanding a slightly higher swing plane. Woods are numbered from 1 to 5, with a 1-wood (or driver) usually having a loft from between 7 to 11°. Low-numbered clubs send the ball further, although they don't lift it as much as high-numbered clubs. A high-numbered club also creates more backspin, which reduces roll on landing. You are allowed a maximum of 14 clubs in your bag, although beginners often make do with a reduced set, say a 2-wood, a 3-, 5-, 7- and 9-iron, and a single wedge.

Below: Irons range from the 2-iron with a loft of 18° to the sand-wedge with 58°.

ANY OLD IRON?

The traditional iron has most of the weight concentrated behind the middle of the

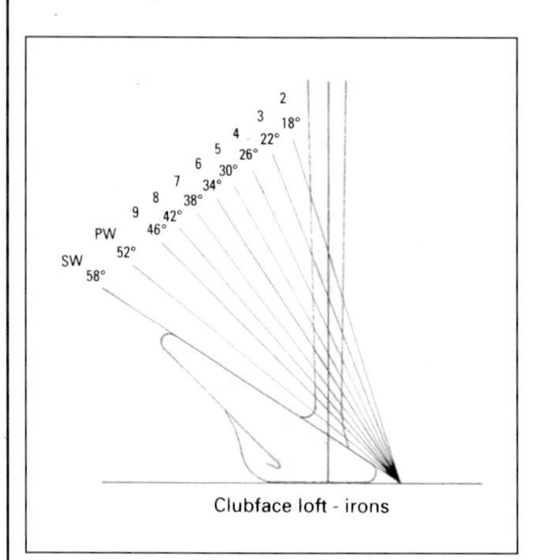

Right: These are the average distances a good player should be able to reach with each club. You should spend time on the practice range to work out the real distances you are capable of achieving.

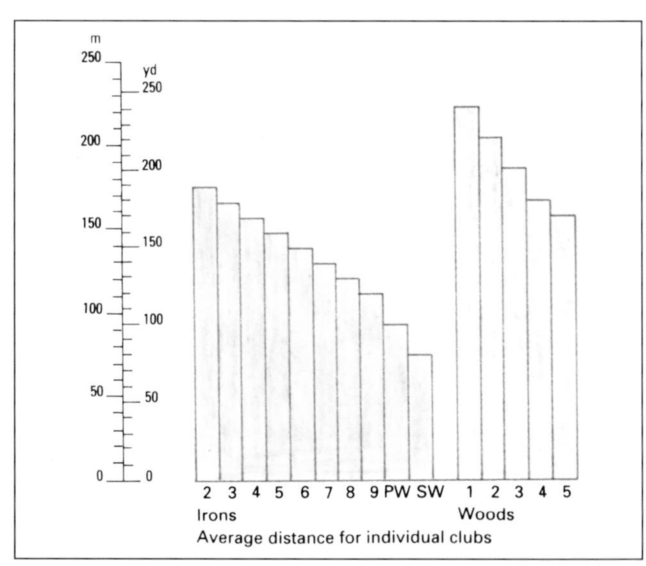

clubface. This central area is known as the sweet spot, and a good, accurate strike here produces a penetrating, powerful flight. The disadvantage is that a slight mishit gives a very poor result. This is an unforgiving style of club, but is used by the majority of professionals and skilled players, who value the precision and control it gives.

An alternative is the peripheral-weighted club, also known as the cavity-backed or game-improvement club. This is designed to be more forgiving, with its weight distributed more evenly around the clubface, effectively increasing the size of the hitting area. If you hit a shot off, say the toe-end, the result won't be so alarmingly different to one struck from the middle. Hence, peripheral-weighted clubs are best for the beginner or inconsistent player. Note though, that many of the world's best players also use these clubs, so don't feel

Above: The traditional iron has its weight in the centre of the clubface, concentrated on a small 'sweet spot'.

Below: The peripheral-weighted club has most mass distributed around the edge of the clubface.

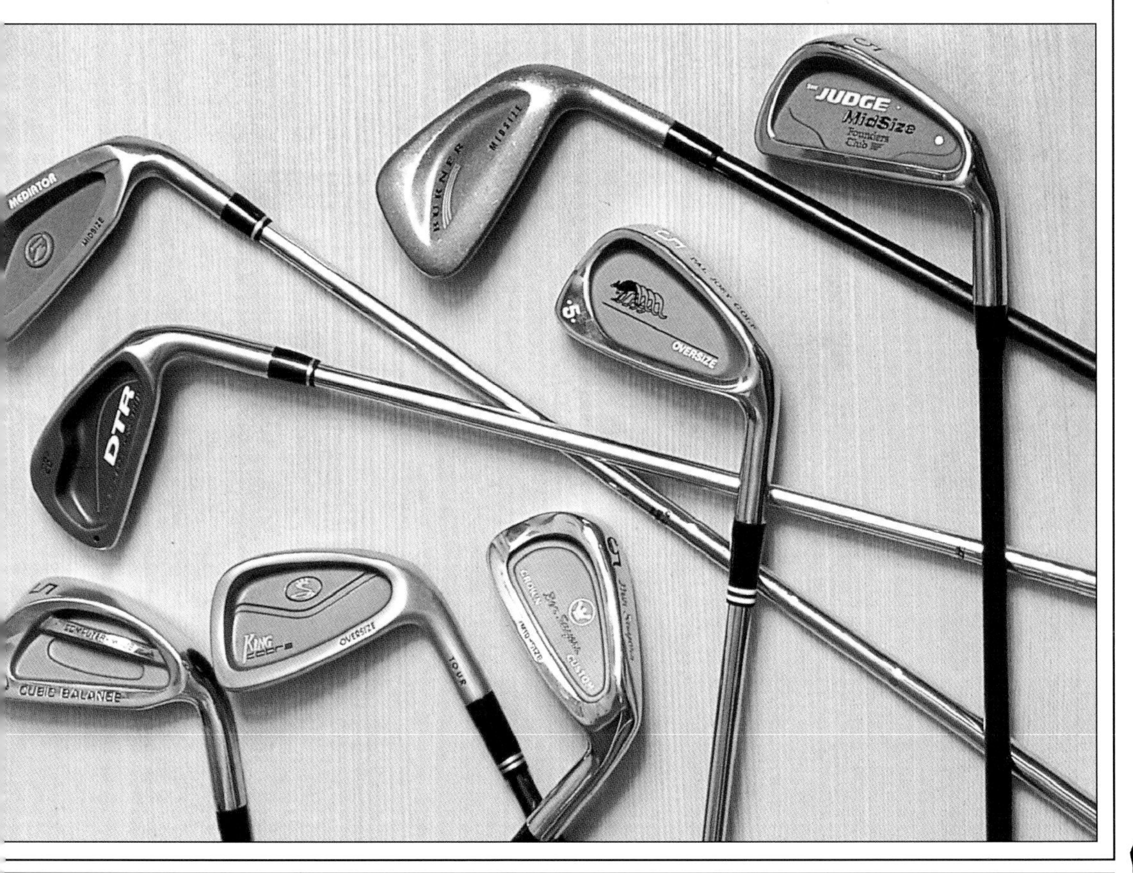

that you are pigeon-holed into any particular category of player when it comes to choosing irons.

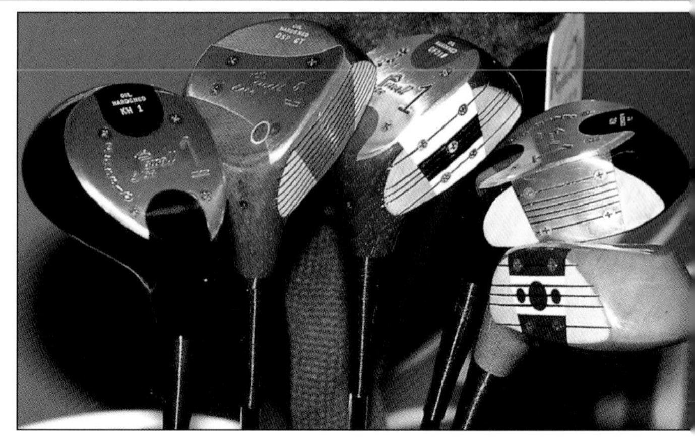

Wood gives the skilled player more control of spin and flight.

METAL AND WOOD

The wood is the long hitter in your golf bag, and can be used from the tee or the fairway. Wood is the traditional, and original, material used in the production of these clubs, and is still favoured by many who play golf at the highest level. Those who use a wooden driver speak of the control and workability it offers - they can shape their shots more readily and prefer the sound and feel that wood offers at impact.

Like the traditional irons, wooden clubs are unforgiving to any inconsistency in your shot. Advances in material design during the last 20 years have seen the development of 'woods' made from a lightweight metal shell, and these now dominate the amateur game. They were originally shaped like their wooden predecessors, but have since metamorphosed into all kinds of shapes and sizes. Their hollow shells allow a greater distribution of weight across the clubhead surface, and offer similar benefits to the peripherally-weighted iron. On the

A range of metal woods, showing various styles of underside, each claimed to give a benefit in performance terms.

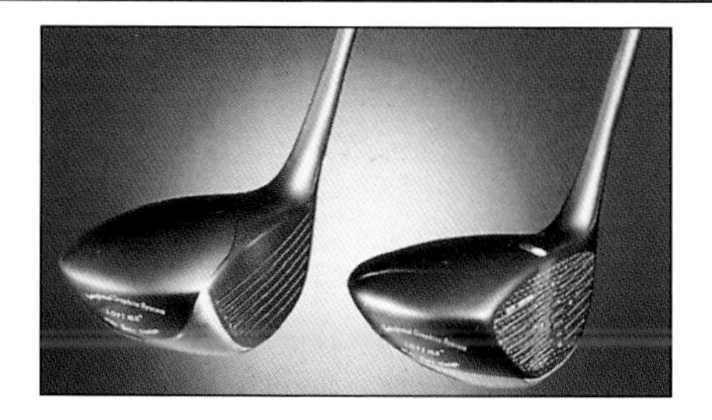

Graphite is claimed to give the best performance from a clubhead design.

downside, though, many good players do not use a metal driver because they feel it is more difficult to shape and control the ball.

Graphite clubheads offer even greater benefits, although they are beyond the pocket of most golfers. As with everything in the golf equipment market, trial and error is absolutely essential. If a club does wonders for your confidence and driving ability, who's to say it isn't worth the money?

THE SHAFT

The importance of what's between your hands and the clubhead is much understated. Not by people who know the game, though. Shafts basically come in three flexes - soft, regular and stiff. As a rule, the better and stronger the player, the stiffer the shaft required. Most amateur players require a soft or regular flex. There are also various types of shaft material available. Steel remains the preferred choice, but graphite does offer significant benefits, albeit at a price. Stronger but lighter than steel, graphite enables manufacturers to concentrate more mass in the clubhead where you need it most.

PUTTERS - A PURELY PERSONAL CHOICE

Appropriately referred to as the game within a game, putting is open to greater personal interpretation than any other aspect of golf. It should therefore come as no surprise that

Shafts are made from steel or graphite, and can be in different grades of flex.

Putters come in a variety of shapes and sizes. Note the grooved line at the top of each clubhead to help alignment with the sweet spot.

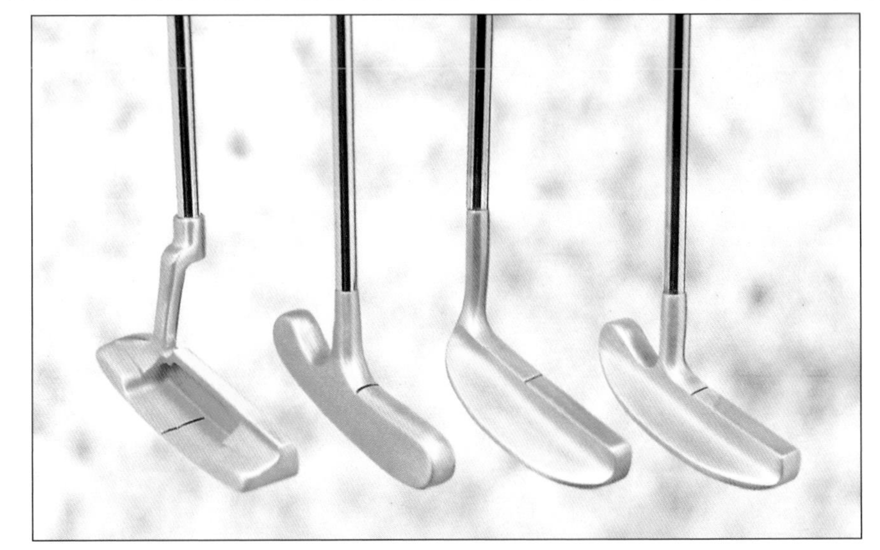

Some players still prefer the traditional bladed putter, whether made from metal or even wood.

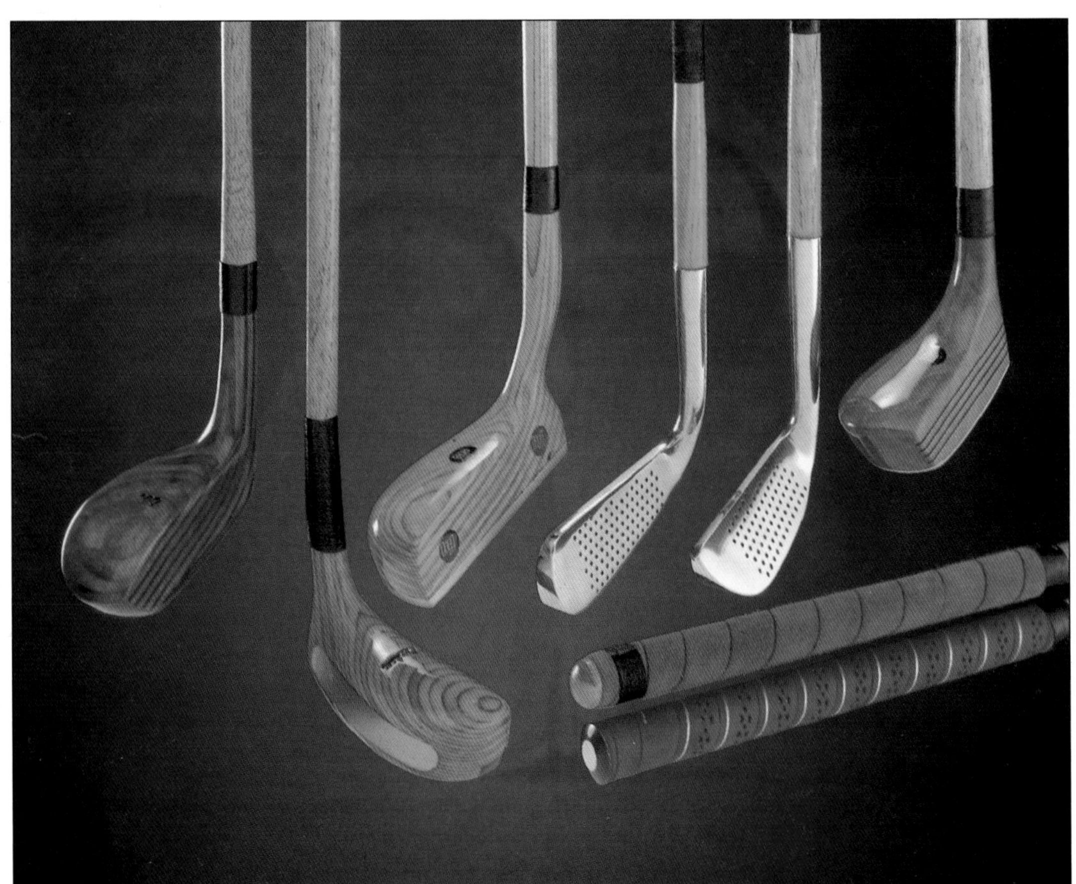

the putter itself is available in a seemingly limitless variety of styles and designs. What started its evolutionary life as the plainest club in the bag is now anything but.

More so than with any other club, choosing a putter is a matter of trial and error, experience and feel. Most modern designs have the weight evenly distributed across the clubface, while many have a kink in the shaft just above the head to encourage your hands to lead the ball. Putting is an unpredictable art at the best of times, and golfers who have used one design of club for many years will be tempted to change when their form suddenly deserts them. Maybe the next club will be the one to revolutionise your performance on the green . . .

CHOOSING THE RIGHT BALL

Different types of ball are geared to suit players of different ability, although you should experiment with all types and choose the one that feels right for you. Professionals use a three-piece ball, with a rubber centre, a wound rubber interior and a separate outer cover. Some have a soft balata cover, which offers maximum spin rate and controllability at the expense of distance, and are chosen by skilled players concerned with feel, touch and control. They are

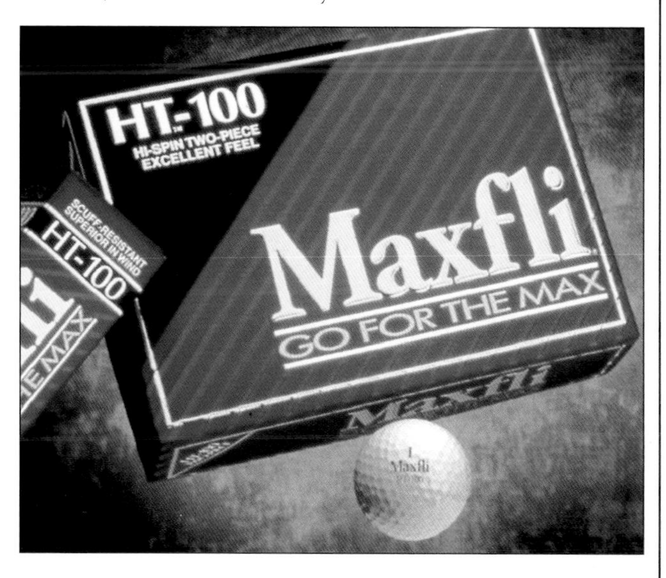

Above and below: These high-compression two-piece balls will give maximum distance to a strong player.

A full-sized professional's bag can easily hold all your equipment and waterproof clothing, but you really need the services of a trolley or caddie.

A lightweight can be carried on the shoulder, and is ideal for good weather conditions.

expensive, however, and easily damaged by a mishit. Other three-pieces come with a tougher surlyn cover, and give a reasonable level of controllability combined with resilience and distance. Most makes are also available in two levels of compression, 90 or 100. The 100 is slightly harder, and is often used by stronger players.

The two-piece ball has a solid rubber centre and a surlyn cover. Durable and tough, this ball drives the furthest, although at the expense of controllability. It is often used by beginners until they have developed their consistency and ball-control skills.

BAGS FOR ALL SEASONS

The type of golf bag you use obviously doesn't have a direct influence on how you play, but it can make a difference to your score at the end of the day. Before you buy a golf bag, throw in some clubs and test how comfortable the strap feels on your shoulder. Many of the lightweight bags on the market are ideal for the summer, but they often don't come with a rain hood, so always have a back-up bag for those rainy days. The professional tour bag is perfect for wet weather, but is obviously too heavy to carry yourself. A trolley, or willing and able caddie, is therefore essential.

DRESS FOR THE OCCASION

If you consider what is involved in a single game of golf, the importance of decent shoes cannot fail to impress. You're likely to walk some four miles (further if your tee shots are off line!) constantly climbing up and down hills with 40lbs of equipment on your back. Not quite army training, but close. You need shoes that are comfortable, waterproof and

Comfortable, waterproof shoes with spiked soles are essential to give a firm foundation to your swing.

that provide adequate support and grip. The most expensive are all-leather, although they do not cope particularly well in wet weather. Some players make do with ribbed soles, but if you are at all serious about golf, you need spiked soles for maximum stability.

Dress codes vary from one golf club to the next, although most find denim jeans, track suits and/or collarless T-shirts unacceptable. If you are visiting a course for the first time, a simple phone call in advance, either to the secretary or the club professional, will avoid any embarrassment or disappointment.

You also need to be able to remain comfortable in poor weather. If you wear a glove, then make sure you carry a few spare in a water-tight plastic bag. No amount of effort will keep your first glove dry for long, so it's important to be able to switch to a dry glove whenever necessary. You need your grips to remain as dry as possible, so keep a towel in the same plastic bag as the gloves to dry them prior to a shot. Also hang a smallish towel in the spokes of your umbrella, so that you can dry your hands, or your grips, at any time. Most golf bags have a drainage hole in the base, so to further ensure that your grips stay dry, plunge a towel down into the bottom of the bag to stop water seeping through. And if your bag comes with a rain hood, make the most of it. Finally, think of yourself, and carry lightweight waterproofs, which will keep you warm and dry while leaving you free to swing. A peaked cap is also useful, or perhaps a visor - especially if you need to keep the rain off spectacles.

With lightweight waterproofs, umbrella, towel and visor, the well-dressed golfer is ready to brave the elements.

CHAPTER 2

Etiquette in golf means more than just a hand-shake. The term encompasses a whole set of principles for showing consideration to your fellow players and to the course. Failure to observe these codes of conduct is one of the most common pitfalls for the beginner, so you should be aware of a few simple rules from the first moment you step onto a course. To help you, here is a short guide to correct golfing behaviour.

THE NICETIES OF **ETIQUETTE**

● 'Look after the golf course and the golf course will look after you' or so the saying goes. In the real world, this doesn't always hold true - but that's not the issue here. Failure to repair damage to the golf course during a round is unforgivable. If you have ever experienced the frustration of having to play from a footmark in a bunker or from a divot in the fairway, you will probably have stronger words of your own to describe those who fail to look after the course.

TAKE CARE OF THE COURSE

FOOTPRINTS IN THE SAND

1 △ One of the most annoying mistakes is when someone leaves footprints and club marks behind in a sand bunker. Before exiting a bunker, always smooth the marks you have made with the rake provided.

2 △ Do not just walk straight up the face of the bunker and continue to play on. If there is no rake, try and use your club as best you can. The ideal is to leave the bunker in the same state in which you would wish to find it.

HOLES IN THE FAIRWAY

1 ◁ It is easy to accidentally lift a divot in the fairway, whether as a result of a practice swing or proper shot.

2 △ You should always take the time to retrieve the divot and replace it in the hole you have created.

3 △ Once it is in place, tread it down securely. In time the grass will naturally repair itself. Note that this treatment isn't necessary in the rough.

● Unrepaired damage to the course is bad enough, but even small bumps and depressions can greatly affect play on the putting surface. It takes many hours of work to keep a green in good condition, but only a few moments' thoughtlessness to spoil it.

KEEP THE GREEN CLEAN

REPAIR YOUR PITCH MARKS

1 ▷ When a pitched ball lands on the green, it usually leaves a small mark or indentation where it lands. You must repair these pitch marks, either with a tee-peg or a tool specifically designed for the purpose.

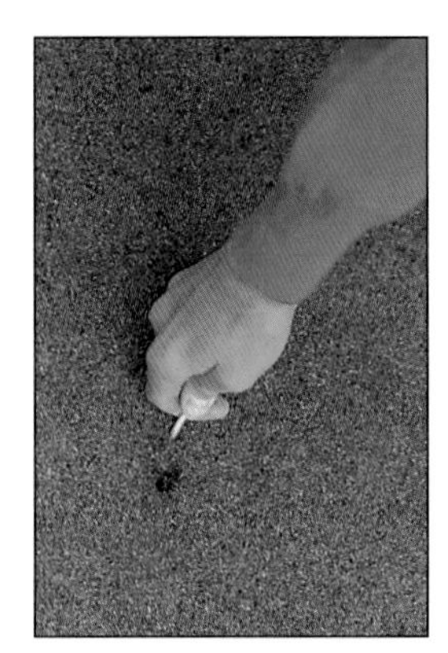

2 △ You then tap the repair down with your putter, which ensures that the damage heals overnight.

3 △ Agronomy studies have shown that it takes at least 21 days for an untreated pitch mark to fully recover. So while you're repairing your own pitch mark, look for any others at the same time. You can be sure someone will have left one behind.

SPIKE MARKS

Spike marks on the line of play cannot be repaired, so you should try to avoid dragging your shoes on the green in such a way that might cause damage.

PLACE THE PIN

1 △ When on the green, always place the flag down gently. Don't throw or drop it.

2 ▽ It doesn't take much abuse for a carefully prepared putting surface to show severe signs of wear and tear.

● Golf is a social game, where you normally play a round with other people, whether as opponents or simply as playing partners. They are entitled to play without any hindrance or irritation caused by thoughtlessness on your part. A few simple actions on your part can help ensure that others enjoy their golf as much as you do.

COURTESY AND COMMON SENSE

THE PLACE TO BE

1 △ Golf is difficult enough without distractions, so when someone is playing a stroke, stand behind them and slightly to the right, out of their eye-line.

2 ▷ If the player is left-handed, you need to stand slightly to their left instead. But whatever way they swing, don't stand directly behind your partner.

3 ▷ You need to think of safety as well as courtesy, by making sure you are not standing too close when your partner is taking his shot.

4 ▽ When on the green, make every effort not to walk across the line of another player's putt.

SLOW PLAY

One of the biggest problems in club golf, and one that can quickly bring down the wrath of other players on the beginner, is that of slow play. While you don't want to rush your shot, there are a few steps you can take to speed your progress around the course.

While your partner is playing their shot, don't just stand there and idly watch. Instead you should be thinking about and preparing for your own shot, so you can play immediately afterwards. After a tee shot, try to walk from the tee directly to your ball - not via your playing partners' balls. Once at the green, another tip is to leave your golf bag on the same side as the next tee - you can then collect it on your way.

If your ball goes into rough, and appears to be well hidden, you should ask any players behind to play through. Don't waste time searching - wave them through immediately. It's easier in the long run and prevents delays and frayed tempers on the tee behind. And don't be ashamed - even top players such as Seve Ballesteros occasionally lose a ball.

CHAPTER 3

Putting is a little bit like religion - there are a multitude of beliefs but no general consensus as to which is the right one. Ben Crenshaw, winner of the 1984 US Masters, is without doubt one of the greatest putters of all time. But even given the remarkable results that Crenshaw's stroke produces, to preach only his method in an instruction book would be telling part of the story - but not all of it.

The best we can do is offer a variety of proven methods and then leave you to select the one that pops the ball into the hole most often. Devote time on the practice green to finding a technique that is right for you. You won't regret it.

PUTTING
THE GAME WITHIN A GAME

● It is never a bad idea to follow the orthodox approach to any sport and this is certainly true of golf. While putting is open to great personal interpretation, it still pays to adhere to the fundamentals. If necessary you can always write your own script, adapted from those principles, to suit yourself.

THE BENEFITS OF **THE ORTHODOX APPROACH**

3 △ The stroke itself is essentially a pendulum action controlled predominantly by the shoulders, with the hands remaining fairly passive. Note the imaginary triangle formed by the arms and shoulders at address.

4 △ Now try to maintain that triangular relationship throughout the stroke, from backswing to final follow-through.

1 ▷ If there is a classic orthodox putting stroke, then this could be said to be it. The hands are placed in a neutral position - the palms facing one another - in what is known as the reverse overlap grip. This encourages the hands to operate as one cohesive unit, rather than have them moving independently of one another.

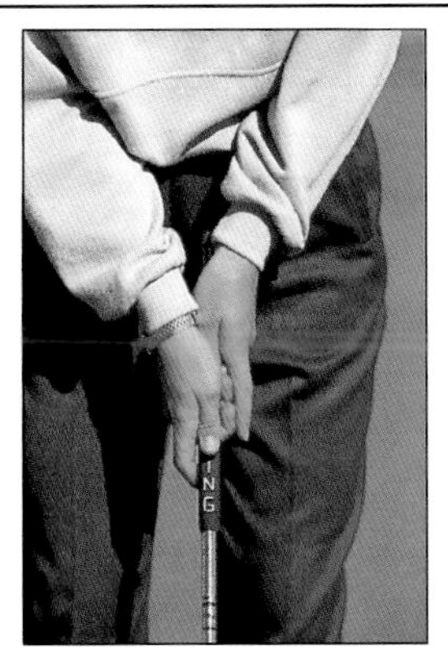

2 ◁ The posture is relaxed - a comfortable bend from the waist with the hands and arms hanging down naturally and completely free from tension. Place the ball forward in your stance, roughly opposite the inside of the left heel. Stand with your eyes positioned over the ball, which allows you to swivel your head to look along the line of the putt.

5 △ You should concentrate on trying to swing the putter-head upwards into and through impact. Having the ball forward in your stance encourages that upward strike and promotes a good roll. On the other hand, a descending blow tends to cause the ball to jump into the air.

6 △ Finally, hold your follow-through position and don't look up too soon. Keep your eyes on the ground until the ball is well on its way. Hopefully, you'll be greeted with the sight of the ball dropping gently into the hole.

● One of the worst faults in putting is allowing the left wrist to 'break down' through impact. Famously referred to as 'the yips', it causes the putter-face to behave erratically - which is bad news for your scorecard.

THE ANTI-YIP STROKE
DROPPING THE LEFT HAND

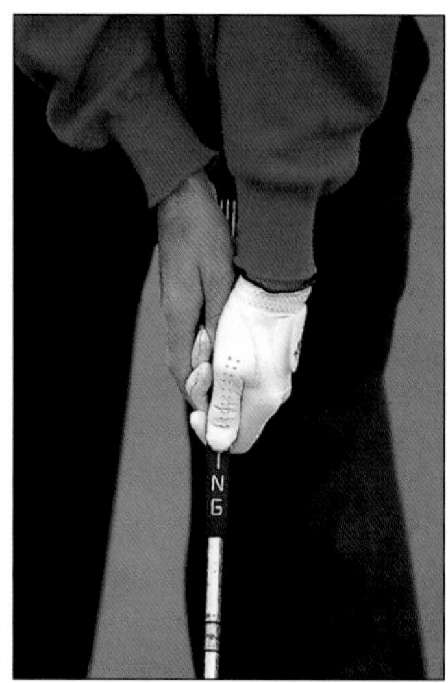

1 △ A basic anti-yip technique is to grip the club with your left hand below the right. This locks the left wrist into position against the shaft of the putter and prevents any unwanted wrist action in the stroke.

2 ▷ This grip also has the added advantage of lowering the left shoulder, bringing it more into line with the right.

3 ◁ Other than that, the stroke is pretty much the same as the more orthodox action described on the previous page.

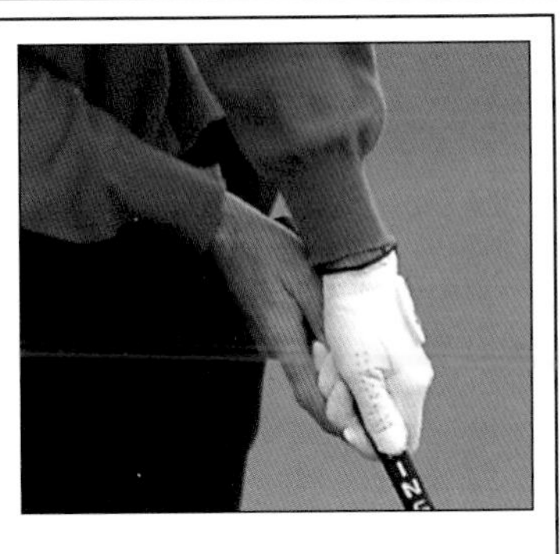

5 △ Again, it's worth emphasising how the left wrist remains firm through the ball. Note how there is no breakdown in this area whatsoever. ▽

4 △ The shoulders control the motion - simply rock them back and forth to regulate the necessary force in the stroke.

● Bernhard Langer has made this method his own and it is the culmination of years of frustration trying to overcome the yips. Since then many other golfers, professional and amateur, have followed Langer's lead. When considering this method, it is as well to know that it is suited mostly to short range putting and is not so effective from long distances.

THE 'LANGER' GRIP
KEEPING THE WRIST LOCKED

3 △ Again, the ideal ball position is opposite the inside of your left heel. Make sure that your grip pressure is light. Any tension here destroys all hope of developing a smooth, repeating stroke.

4 △ From here, simply concentrate on rocking your shoulders back and through. This should provide all the force in the stroke.

1 ▷ Assume a comfortable stance and place the putter-head behind the ball, aiming the clubface using your right hand only.

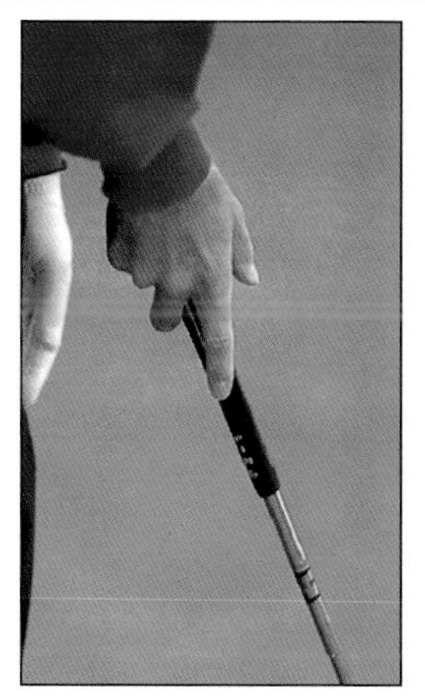

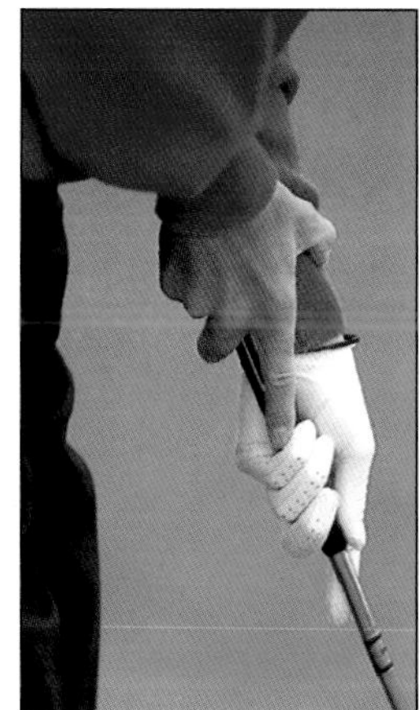

2 ◁ Reach down with your left hand, gripping the club in a fairly orthodox manner, and clasp the fingers of your right hand around your left forearm, rather like you would do to take your own pulse. This effectively takes the right hand out of the stroke.

5 △ The hands remain fairly passive and there is no wrist action whatsoever.

6 △ The putter should move back and through in a straight line, staying square throughout with no interference from the hands.

● This specially modified long putter aroused much controversy when Sam Torrance first used it in the late 1980s. Gradually, though, it has become seen as a viable way to putt, as is evident by the fact that some of the world's professionals have taken it up to good effect.

Even though it does look a little strange, there are benefits to this style, which hinges on the principle that you recreate a perfect pendulum motion with the putter.

USING THE LONG PUTTER
TORRANCE'S PERFECT PENDULUM

Sam Torrance's specially extended putter helped improve his consistency.

1 ◁ Grip the club in your left hand at the top of the putter and secure it in position against either your chin or chest, depending on the length of the shaft.

3 ▷ The beauty of this method is that you let the weight and momentum of the putter do all the work for you. And the fact that the right hand guides the stroke means that there is no chance of your hands working independently of one another.

2 △ Now it is simply a case of gripping the club lightly in your right hand, rather as you would a pencil, and rocking the putter-head smoothly back and forth.

'The weight and momentum of the putter does all the work for you'

4 △ A strange method, yes. But it did wonders for Sam Torrance, and you never know, it might work for you.

COMMON COMPLAINT

One of the biggest causes of missed putts is looking up too soon. It's usually caused out of anxiety, particularly when hitting from short range. You're desperate to know if the ball is going in - sadly, if you peek too soon, it seldom does.

PEEKING TOO SOON

1 ◁ The reason you miss putts in this way lies in a simple chain reaction. If you move your head too soon, then your whole upper body moves with it, which effectively drags the putter-face left of the target at impact. The result? Crooked putts every time.

CLASSIC CURE

It's worth stressing that changing your routine takes time to get used to. Familiarise yourself with this technique on the practice green before trying it on the course.

WAIT FOR THE TELL-TALE SOUND

Next time you're on the practice green, get used to not looking up until you hear the sound of the ball dropping into the hole. From anywhere inside five or six feet, discipline yourself to hit the putt and wait for the tell-tale sound. Your stroke is guaranteed to stay on line for longer. And when you do finally look up, you'll see that the ball has dropped in the hole a lot more often than before.

1 △ For something a little bit different, set up a medium range putt and address the ball. Now close your eyes.

2 △ Keeping the eyes closed, stroke the ball towards the hole.

3 △ This prevents you becoming too pre-occupied with hitting at the ball and, more importantly, helps you concentrate on making a smooth stroke

4 △ Note the constant emphasis on the word 'smoothly'. Your stroke should not be a jab at the ball. The perfect stroke is one that takes the putter back low and slow, smoothly accelerating through impact. The ball merely gets in the way.

COMMON COMPLAINT

A smooth continuous action is essential, no matter what style of stroke or grip you use. The pressure of trying to get the ball into that tiny hole can easily cause you to tense up or rush your shot.

DECELERATION THROUGH IMPACT

1 ◁ The length of your backswing is crucial when it comes to striking good putts. The most destructive error of all is taking the club too far back.

2 ▷ You then tend to decelerate in the downswing and jab the ball with almost no follow-through. When you start doing that you can forget about even getting the ball anywhere near the hole, let alone sinking the putt.

CLASSIC CURE

It doesn't matter how short the putt, or how fast the green, you must accelerate the putter-head into the back of the ball to stand any chance of holing out on a consistent basis. As a simple rule of thumb, always ensure that your throughswing is exactly the same length as your backswing. Then concentrate on smoothly accelerating the putter through the ball.

ACCELERATE SMOOTHLY THROUGH THE BALL

1 ◁ Try this practice drill. Place two tee-pegs in the ground the same distance either side of your ball. The longer the putt then the longer the clearance you need between the ball and the tee-pegs.

2 ◁ Hit some putts and use the tee-pegs to regulate the length of your stroke.

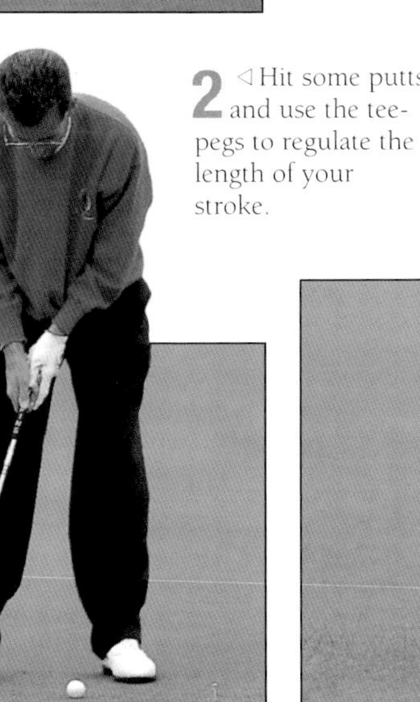

3 ◁ Concentrate on smoothly accelerating the putter-head through impact, whilst making sure that your backswing is exactly the same length as your follow-through.

CHAPTER 4

THE FUNDAMENTALS

THE BUILDING BLOCKS OF GOLF

The fundamentals are the basis of a long-lasting, successful golf swing. They may seem trivial, perhaps even dull at times, but the importance of grip, set-up and posture cannot be exaggerated.

If you were to take a browse around the practice grounds of the world's best tournaments you would see top class players paying most of their attention to the pre-swing factors. They are well aware that most faults in golf can be traced back to an incorrect address position. Any golfer who ignores these fundamentals is effectively waving goodbye to a solid, reliable golf swing.

● The legendary golfer Ben Hogan summed it up perfectly when he said; 'A player with a bad grip doesn't want a good swing.'

There are three basic types of grip. The overlapping, which is the most popular method; the interlocking, which tends to be favoured by golfers with relatively short fingers; and the two-handed, or baseball grip as it is often referred to, which is ideal for juniors or players who have arthritic problems.

FORMING THE PERFECT GRIP

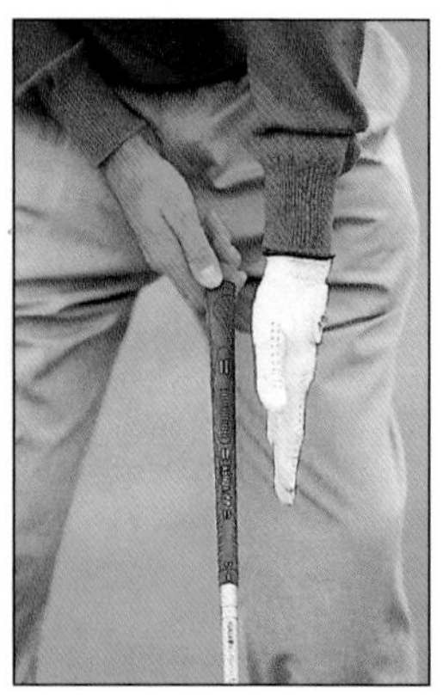

1 △ Support the top of the club with your right hand. Hang the left hand naturally down the side of the grip.

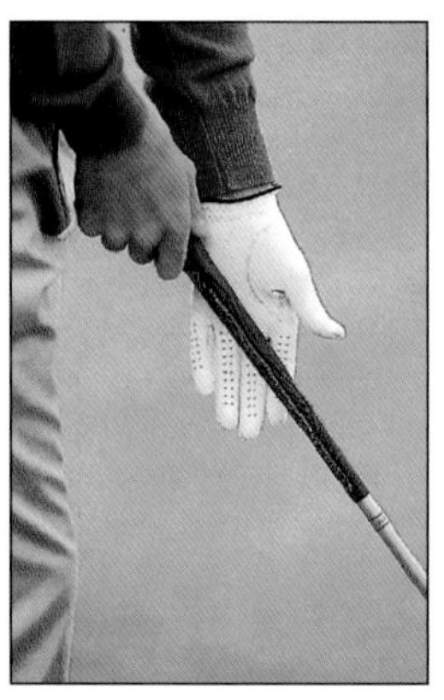

2 △ Bring your left hand forward from its natural hanging position and hold it against the grip in such a way that the shaft runs from the fleshy pad in your palm down diagonally through the middle joint of your index finger.

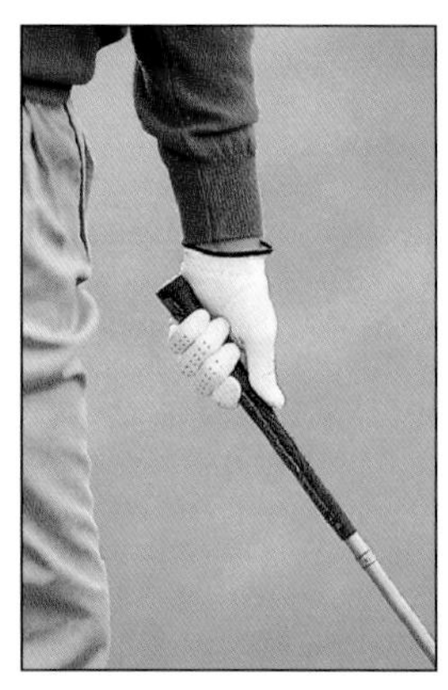

3 △ Now close the fingers of your left hand around the club.

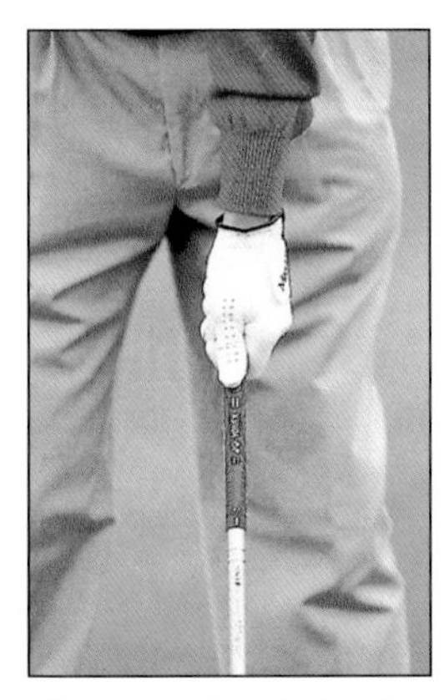

4 △ Your thumb should be flat on the grip, perhaps a little to the right of centre as you look down on it.

'Your hands are the only contact with the club, so it had better be good contact'

The interlocking grip

The overlapping grip

The baseball grip

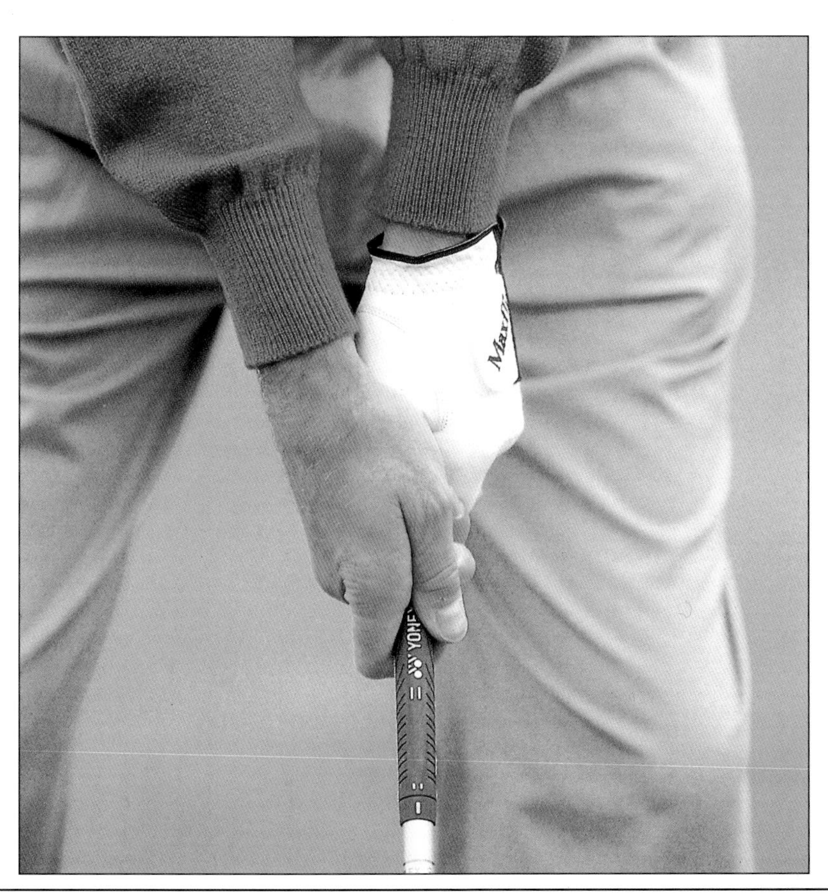

5 ◁ Now bring your right hand forward, again from its natural hanging position, and lay the club in the fingers of that hand. Try to imagine that your right palm coincides with the angle of the clubface, in other words is square to the target. Your right thumb and forefinger should form a kind of trigger around the grip, almost to the extent that you can support the weight of the club in your finger and thumb. At the same time bond the little finger of your right hand in whichever way you feel is comfortable, in either interlocking, overlapping, or baseball style.

● It almost goes without saying that you can't expect to hit a target if you point the gun in the wrong direction. Likewise you can't hit consistently good golf shots if your set-up is incorrect. It just doesn't work.

SET FOR ACTION

△ PERFECT PARALLEL ALIGNMENT
Parallel alignment is the key factor and it works like this. Imagine a railway track running from your position to the target. The outer rail runs along the ball-to-target line, and is where you should align your clubface. The inner rail runs along the line through your feet, and ends up just to the left of the target. If you line your feet and club along these imaginary tracks, you will be in perfect parallel alignment.

◁ BALL POSITION
Parallel alignment is the precursor to good golf shots, but it's only part of the story. You also need the ball correctly positioned in the stance to ensure that the clubhead collects it on the ideal path. So what is the best ball position? Well, it varies depending on which club you are hitting.

The relatively straight face of the driver means that you must sweep the ball away to achieve decent results. That's why you need the ball forward in your stance, roughly opposite the inside of your left heel, so that the club reaches the bottom of its swing at impact.

Short irons are different. They call for a more descending angle of attack - the clubhead must be travelling downwards into impact to ensure that you achieve ideal ball-then-turf contact. It therefore makes sense that with the short irons the ball should be positioned back in your stance, pretty much midway between your feet.

A SECURE POSTURE

The term posture refers to the body angles you create at address. Good posture gives you a head-start and actively encourages a good shape to your swing. As you stand over the ball you should feel ready to go, and poised to swing the club away from the ball. Conversely, if your posture is poor, you're making the game of golf even harder than it already is.

2 ◁ Bend forward from the hips allowing your hands and arms to hang down comfortably. Flex your knees and stick out your rear-end slightly. Your stance should feel powerful, almost athletic. If someone were to shove you from behind or the side, you wouldn't lose your balance.

1 △ This routine will allow you to assume perfect posture every time. Once you have your feet in position, stand upright, with a club resting by your side.

3 ▽ Now reach for the club (or have someone hand it to you) without altering any of the angles you create at address, and simply ground the club. It might feel a little strange at first, but you've now established the perfect posture for someone of your height and build. You've made a huge step towards building a sound golf swing.

COMMON COMPLAINT

Golfers are traditionally lazy about their grip. It isn't an exciting subject so it doesn't tend to receive the attention that it warrants. Sadly, many golfers who grip the club badly do so out of ignorance, which can be prevented by a few minutes'study. There are two main types of poor grip, both of which make it extremely difficult to return the clubface square to the ball at impact.

WEAK AND STRONG GRIPS

1 ▷ The two types of poor grip are referred to as weak and strong. Your grip is weak if your hands are turned too far round to the left.

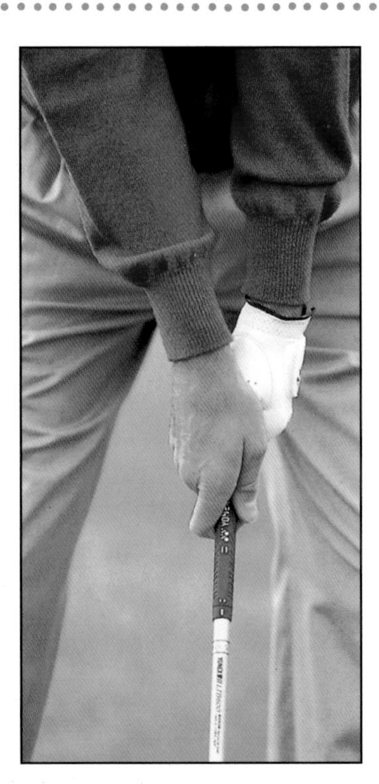

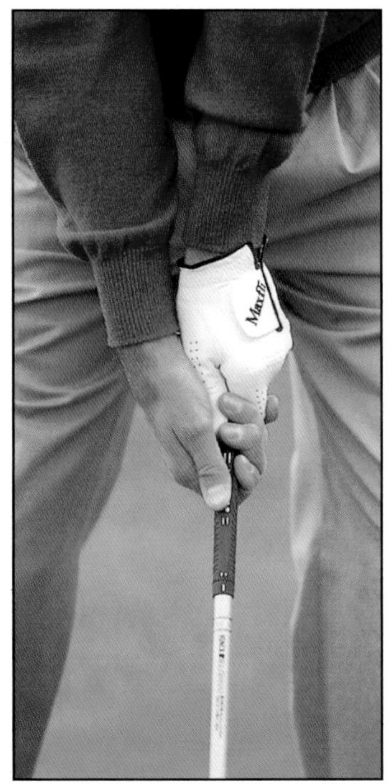

2 ◁ Your grip is strong if your hands are turned too far to the right. A slightly strong right hand grip is acceptable, but from the front you should never be able to see more than three knuckles.

CLASSIC CURE

If your shots are flying off-line don't necessarily look to your swing for the cure. Your grip influences your impact position, so go straight to the root cause and look at the position of your hands. Ideally, both hands should be in a neutral position. Here is a simple way to check that this is indeed the case.

V FOR VICTORY

1 △ Stand in front of a mirror and slowly place each hand on the grip. First the left hand. As you look at it, the 'V' formed by the index finger and thumb should point up somewhere between your right eye and right shoulder.

2 ▷ Similarly with the right hand, the 'V' should point to the same area between your right eye and right shoulder. If there's any deviation from this, your hands are in the wrong position.

COMMON COMPLAINT

Your legs are the foundation of your swing; they stabilise and support the rotary action of your body as it winds and unwinds through the ball. So you must have the correct amount of flex in your knees. Likewise, you must create the correct body angles before you can hope to build a good swing. Like any structure, if the foundations are faulty then the upper reaches have a tendency to crumble.

LEGS AND BODY ANGLES

1 ▷ Too much flex in the knees is rare, but it does happen.

2 ◁ One thing is certain, there aren't too many good swings made from this position.

1 ▷ Rigid, straight legs at address are a more familiar sight.

2 ◁ Again, from here it is impossible to make a powerful turn away from the ball.

CLASSIC CURE

You must learn not only to feel the correct amount of flex in your knees, but also to create the ideal body angles at address. If you are unsure about your posture, rehearse this simple drill.

FEEL THE FLEX

1 △ Address the ball as you would normally and then hold the shaft of a club along the length of your spine. Get used to the feeling of sticking out your rear-end slightly and matching the angle of your spine with the line of the shaft of the club.

2 ◁ Repeat this exercise as many times as you like and familiarise yourself with the sensation that it brings. As you begin to feel more comfortable with the position, start to hit half-shots.

3 △ Now you've established a solid foundation, it will make it easier to arrive in a good position at the top of the backswing and continue the good work from there.

CHAPTER 5

THE PRECISE ART OF CHIPPING

At club level much emphasis is placed on the importance of building a sound golf swing, but this very worthwhile goal is often sought at the expense of the short game. This certainly isn't the case at the highest level. Colin Montgomerie will probably devote as much time to working on the short game as he will to the full swing. The big Scot is well aware that the sheer variety of situations that can confront him in a tournament will test his chipping skills to the extreme.

Close to the green is an area where imagination and versatility are essential qualities. First, though, you need to understand the necessary techniques involved. Then, through practice, you can set about developing your feel for those all-important shots around the green. This chapter will help you on both fronts.

● It's important that you understand, and master, the stock chip shot before you even think about playing any of the more fancy shots around the green. Once you do you'll discover the same technique can be applied to a number of different clubs, thus creating a whole repertoire of shots to suit a variety of situations. Here's how it is done.

THE STANDARD CHIP

A VERSATILE SHOT

1 △ As is the case with every golf shot, your address position is a vital factor. Adopt an open stance with your feet fairly close together and your weight favouring the left side. A useful term to remember is, 'ball back, hands forward and weight forward'.

2 △ Now, keeping your weight exactly where it is, make a compact backswing.

3 △ Wrist break is fairly minimal - you just need a slight hinging, or setting, of the wrists as you complete the backswing. This effectively keeps the hands in charge, in an ideal position to lead the clubhead down into the ball.

'Ball back hands forward and weight forward'

5 ▷ Again, it is worth emphasising the fact that your hands should stay ahead of the clubhead even through impact. This technique is very versatile and thus can be used to good effect with your 7-iron, 9-iron and sand-wedge. Through experience and practice you will soon learn which clubs perform best in certain situations.

4 △ At impact, you should feel that the ball is compressed between the clubface and turf. It is this sensation of squeezing the ball forward towards the target which helps produce the necessary backspin. With a lofted club you can expect a good deal of check-spin to retard the ball on the second or third bounce.

● Here's a useful variation on the standard chip shot - it's a sort of hybrid golf shot: part chip and part putt. And it's much simpler than it sounds, too. It's most useful when you have a relatively short distance, say anywhere under 20 yards, but the ground between your ball and the green is a little bumpy.

THE PUTT-CHIP
A SIMPLE ALTERNATIVE

1 ◁ Take a fairly lofted club, something like an 8 or 9-iron, and set up to the ball as if you were preparing to hit a long putt. Place your weight over on the left side and position the ball opposite your left heel. And remember, adopt your normal putting grip. This helps deaden the impact and enables you to control the length of the shot more accurately.

2 △ Now, simply go ahead and focus on making an extension of your normal putting stroke.

'This is a shot that can make a lot of difference around the green'

3 ▷ Make a fairly brisk action and clip the ball away.

4 △ You'll find that the ball is lobbed gently forward, fairly low and with plenty of run.

5 △ It will race towards the hole, just like a long putt.

● This is a shot that you should only play if you really have no other option, the classic example being when there is a bunker between your ball and the flag. If you've lots of green to work with then forget it. There are plenty of other, safer, shots better suited to the task.

THE HIGH-FLOATING LOB SHOT

1 ◁ The best way to describe the high-floater is to say that it is virtually the same as playing from a greenside bunker. First, you need to align your feet, hips and shoulders a little to the left of the target. This is known as an 'open' stance.

2 △ Take your sand-wedge and align the clubface a little to the right of the target. This is known as an 'open' club. Position the ball forward in your stance, roughly opposite the left heel.

3 △ Now for the swing itself. Keep your arm-swing in tune with your body rotation away from the ball, allowing your wrists to hinge gradually all the way through the backswing. This sets you on an ever-so-slightly steeper plane than normal. You may only have a short distance to cover, but you still need to make a relatively long swing, both back and through the ball.

4 ◁ On the way down, maintain the same smoothly accelerating action and almost slide the clubhead through the grass under the ball.

5 ◁ Don't allow any meddling wrist action to creep in - as you rotate your body out of the way through impact, keep your left wrist firm and your right hand under the shaft to ensure that the clubface does not close.

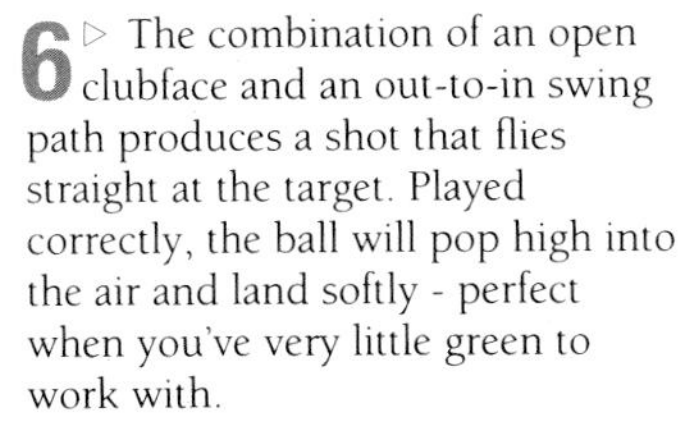

6 ▷ The combination of an open clubface and an out-to-in swing path produces a shot that flies straight at the target. Played correctly, the ball will pop high into the air and land softly - perfect when you've very little green to work with.

'A difficult shot that just might be a game-winner'

●The bare lie on hard ground is perhaps the most feared of all, simply because it seemingly gives you so little margin for error. True, it does call for precise technique. But that's not as demanding as it sounds.

THE CHIP FROM HARD GROUND

1 ▷ In lots of ways, playing off a bare lie demands that you accentuate all the maxims and techniques which relate to the normal chip. The term 'ball back, hands forward and weight forward' is even more critical. You really need to exaggerate each of these three factors by another 20%, so that the ball is well back in your stance and your hands and weight favour the left side even more than normal.

The first thing you need to understand is that your sand-wedge is totally unsuited to the job of playing off a bare lie. The wide flange on the sole of the club raises the leading edge off the ground just a fraction, which is perfect for sand shots. From a bare lie, though, it has a tendency to cause you to clip the top ('thin') the ball.

So always go with a club that has a sharper leading edge, such as a 9-iron. The leading edge sits tighter to the ground and enables you to execute the shot more precisely.

2 △ Now it's a case of making a compact backswing with a hint of wrist-break, and smoothly accelerating the clubhead into the bottom of the ball.

3 △ Once again, the single most important aspect of the shot is to keep your hands ahead of the clubhead into, and through, impact.

4 △ If you can always achieve those impact factors, bare lies should hold few fears for you.

● A good chipper of the ball is someone who combines a solid technique with a keen awareness of the feel factor; in other words, the ability to judge flight, bounce and roll. Once you have a sound grasp of the technique involved, this is a good way to develop your feel. What you are doing is recreating an actual 'on-course' situation. You only get one chance at each shot during a round of golf, so it's good to put yourself under the same kind of pressure when you practise.

DEVELOPING YOUR FEEL FACTOR

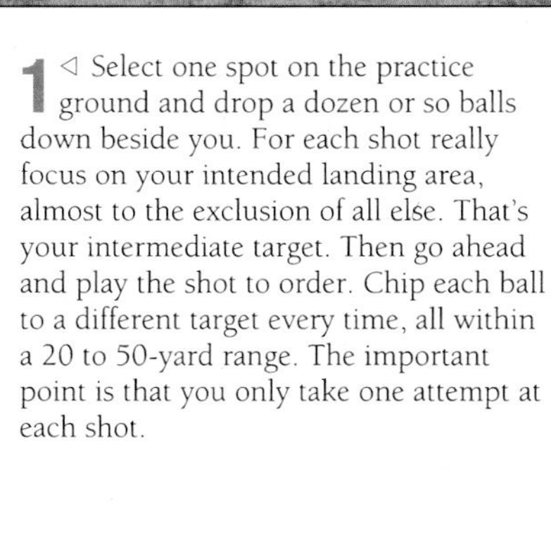

1 ◁ Select one spot on the practice ground and drop a dozen or so balls down beside you. For each shot really focus on your intended landing area, almost to the exclusion of all else. That's your intermediate target. Then go ahead and play the shot to order. Chip each ball to a different target every time, all within a 20 to 50-yard range. The important point is that you only take one attempt at each shot.

2 △ If you don't have a practice green like this, you can use head covers as targets. The whole purpose of this exercise is that you should grow accustomed to visualising each shot before you play it. Select a landing area and predict the amount of run on the ball required, then match the club to fit your assessment. Feel free to experiment with any club between your 7-iron and sand-wedge.

'Self-imposed pressure can be the greatest enemy of the golfer, and learning to overcome it can make a world of difference to your play'

COMMON COMPLAINT

With chipping, particularly over sand, the natural tendency is often to become so concerned with generating height that you scoop at the ball in an attempt to help it into the air. For some, it is simply plain ignorance of the correct technique which lands them in trouble.

SCOOPING THE BALL

1 △ The ball is often positioned too far forward in the stance. The hands are behind the ball, too, which is bound to cause further problems. From this awkward address position, it can only get worse rather than better.

2 ◁ Impact becomes a scooping action with the clubhead travelling upwards into the middle of the ball, sending it scuttling along the ground.

3 △ Tragically, in all your efforts to create height, you manage to perpetrate the exact outcome you were desperately trying to avoid - a bunker shot before your next putt!

CLASSIC CURE

This is where the old golfing adage receives its first airing: 'You've got to hit down to create height.' The sooner you can grasp this concept, and put it into practice, the better your short game will become. Try this exercise.

TRUST THE LOFT TO DO ITS JOB

1 △ Always trust the loft on the clubface to do the job it was designed to do. Set up the shot with the ball in the centre of your stance and your hands comfortably ahead of that point. As a quick check, your left arm and the shaft of the club should form pretty much a straight line down to the ball.

2 ◁ Once established at address, it's important you maintain that relationship throughout the swing. The hands lead the clubhead into the ball to encourage a crisp, downward strike.

3 △ This utilises the effective loft on the clubface and ensures that you create height on the shot. Soon, you will find those embarrassing fluffed chips are consigned to the deep and distant past.

CHAPTER 6

Pitch shots are the in between shots – longer than a chip, but shorter than a full swing. For this reason, they're often played badly. Rather than attacking the pin as they should, many golfers miss the green altogether.

Jose Maria Olazabal is positively deadly from inside 100 yards. He doesn't settle for merely hitting greens - he wants to hole every shot. This ability is reflected in his scores. And, as Gary Player once observed, 70% of all shots in a round of golf are played within 70 yards of the green. All the more reason then to develop a reliable technique in this, one of the most crucial areas on the golf course.

PERFECT **PITCHING**

● If you can master the short game around the green, it will do wonders for your score. But before you can drop those neat pitching shots onto the pin you have to grasp some of the fundamentals. Versatility, judgement and control are all essential prerequisites to fine approach play.

SHARPEN YOUR APPROACH PLAY

A TRIO OF WEDGES

Such are the variety of situations that can confront you around the greens, it is essential you have the necessary equipment on board to give you maximum versatility. Let's remind ourselves again of what Gary Player said; 70% of shots are played from within 70 yards of the green. That's why professional golfers carry three wedges - they know that more often than not they will need every one of them in the space of 18 holes.

For some reason, though, very few club players choose to carry three wedges. If you're one of those golfers, then it's time for a change. There are a huge variety of wedges on the market, ranging from 52° to 60° in loft. If you have three to chose from - say a 52°, a 56° and a 60° - you have the option of playing a wide range of shots at the critical ranges. So even if you already have 14 clubs in your bag (the maximum permitted) you can introduce a third wedge at the expense of one of your longer clubs, such as the 2-iron or 5-wood. It won't take long for you to notice the difference in the sharpness of your approach play - and in your scores.

TOTAL CONTROL

Control, accuracy and judgement of distance are what matter most when you're homing in on the green. It is therefore essential that you do everything you can to enhance that control.

Gripping down on the club is one such measure. This reduces the gap between your hands and the clubhead and effectively shortens your swing in both directions, back and through. It further enhances your control and enables you to make a positive swing, safe in the knowledge that you won't overshoot the target.

THE OPEN STANCE

As with most other aspects of golf, the majority of problems people have with pitching stem from a faulty set-up position. Many players make the mistake of setting up to the ball as they do for a normal full shot; in other words, square to the target line. This immediately causes problems.

The fact that you stand closer to the ball, combined with the shorter shaft of your pitching clubs, means that your swing is naturally more upright. If you adopt a square stance, as you would for a regular full shot, you simply do not have time to clear your left side - you almost get in the way of yourself. You actually need to align yourself slightly to the left of the target line, in an 'open' stance. This helps you clear your left side out of the way in the downswing, thus enabling you to deliver the clubhead square to the ball.

● This is the shot you would use at distances from 70 to 100 yards. Having established the correct address position, you are now in great shape to make a good swing. If you can imagine a three-quarter swing, back and through, then that is a good image to keep in mind.

THE STANDARD PITCH SHOT

1 △ Use your arms and shoulders to swing the club away from the ball in conjunction with the turning motion of your upper body.

2 △ Everything moves away together. Sometimes referred to as 'staying connected in the backswing', this is a far more consistent method than if your hands and arms work independently of the rest of your body.

3 △ Your body rotation should control the length of your backswing, and you need to keep your arms working in harmony to maintain that relationship.

'Perfect this regular pitching technique as best you can and then learn to apply it to a range of clubs'

4 △ Similarly, in the downswing you should consciously make the arms and body control the swing together. Your hands need to stay fairly passive.

5 △ Accelerate the clubhead down into and through impact, with the emphasis on the body, not the hands.

6 △ Practise this technique with a number of clubs, say, your 9-iron, pitching-wedge and sand-wedge. This will enable you to use exactly the same swing without any conscious manipulation, while varying the distance you can hit the ball. That's smart golf.

● This is a situation that all golfers face a little more often than they would wish – your ball is buried in the rough. Sure, there are some things you cannot do out of the rough that you can from the fairway, but there's absolutely no reason why you cannot set yourself up for a holeable putt. The most important thing is to set about creating a steeper angle of attack in order to make the best possible contact with the ball.

PITCHING FROM DEEP ROUGH

1 ◁ The key to achieving this is to position the ball further back in your stance. Doing this means that the clubhead naturally reaches impact before it reaches the bottom of its swing arc, thus minimising the amount of grass trapped between the clubface and the ball.

2 ▷ Hover the clubhead off the ground just a fraction, too. This will also help you hit the ball as cleanly as possible at impact.

3 △ Once you've pre-set this steep angle of attack, take a slightly shorter club than you would from the same distance on the fairway and choke your hands down on the grip.

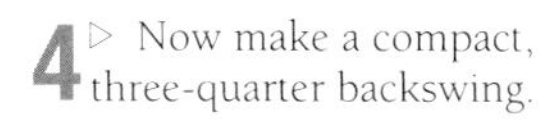

4 ▷ Now make a compact, three-quarter backswing.

5 △ You need to make sure that you punch the clubhead down into the back of the ball.

6 △ Don't expect to generate backspin out of the rough - it just isn't possible - so allow for more run on the ball than you would with a shot from the fairway.

● If either your swing or your strategy is vulnerable, then wind has a nasty habit of exposing these weaknesses. Most golfers try to hit the ball harder, but this creates excessive spin and lift on the ball, which is further exaggerated by the wind. When the wind is blowing hard, the key to keeping your scores low is to keep the ball low.

THE WIND CHEATER

1 △ First establish whether you're dealing with a one-club, two-club or three-club wind. Select your club accordingly and choke down on the grip an inch or two. Judging the strength of the wind, and the effect it has on your ball, is a lesson you can only learn through experience. If you're not totally certain, don't worry, it will come in time. Place the ball centrally in your stance with your hands ahead of the clubhead, perfect for punching the ball out on a low trajectory. Shift your weight slightly over to the left side - a ratio of 60 to 40 is ideal. And remember, your feet should be aligned to the left of the target.

2 △ Now, make a compact, three-quarter backswing with a little less hinging of the wrists than you would normally apply.

3 △ You should keep your swing nicely rounded, again with your arms and body working in unison. Also, don't transfer your weight as much as you would for a full shot. Keep it centred over the ball.

'Place the ball centrally in your stance with your hands ahead of the clubhead'

4 ◁ Now, from a three-quarter position, make sure your hands lead the clubhead down towards the ball. Rotate your upper body and try to keep the clubhead travelling low to the ground through impact and around into a balanced finish.

5 ▽ Note how the follow-through is the same length as the backswing - that's a very constructive image to have in mind. And remember, in the breeze swing with ease. The harder you hit the ball, the more backspin you generate and the higher the ball climbs.

● The main problem most people have with pitching shots is judging and controlling the distance they shoot. A common fault is when the player makes the same length of backswing for all pitch shots, while attempting to regulate distance by varying the amount of force they exert in the downswing. This is an extremely haphazard way of controlling distance and tends to produce inconsistent shots. What you must appreciate is that the length of your backswing should directly relate to the distance the ball flies.

USE 'FOUR GEARS' FOR PITCHING

1 ◁ The best way to visualise this is to imagine that there are four 'gears' to your swing. First gear is the short chip shot.

2 ◁ While fourth gear is when you let fly with a full swing.

In between, then, are second and third gears, which are the gears you use for pitching. So, go to the practice ground or driving range with this in mind. What this exercise does is give you a feeling of how the length of swing relates to the distance you actually hit the ball. You can also apply this exercise to a variety of clubs, for example to give you two different length pitch shots with your 9-iron.

1 ▷ Hit 10 half-shots with your wedge - that's second gear.

2 ◁ Make sure the follow-through is as long as the backswing. Make a note of the average distance your shots travel.

3 ▷ Now hit 10 three-quarter shots - that's third gear. Again note the average 'air time' for every one.

4 ◁ Practise this exercise as often as you can until your second and third gear achieve a reasonable level of consistency. The next time you're on the course and you have, for instance, 75 yards to the flag, you can say to yourself: 'OK, this is third gear with my sand-wedge.' You're removing the guesswork and replacing it with positive, constructive thoughts.

CHAPTER 7

American professional Tom Purtzer is credited by his fellow players as having the best swing in the world of golf. Before you can hope to achieve anything like such classic style, you need to first pay attention to the nuts and bolts of the swing. And a visit to any professional tournament provides ample evidence that text-book style isn't necessary, and that there are many different ways to swing a golf club. But whatever technique they use, all good players have one thing in common - the ability to consistently deliver the clubhead correctly to the ball. If you can manage that, the aesthetics can take care of themselves.

THE FULL SWING

● All good golfers have a consistent pre-shot routine, a series of moves which helps them assume the correct address position and posture every time they stand to the ball. If you need convincing of the importance of the address position, study professionals in action and see how meticulous they are in this area. They are well aware that no matter how well the gun is firing, it must be pointing in the right direction for the bullet to hit the mark. It's essential that you also develop your own set-up routine, ideally based on the following principles.

THE VALUE OF A **PRE-SHOT ROUTINE**

1 △ First, stand behind the ball and visualise the exact shot you want to hit. This helps you focus your mind on the task at hand while fixing the target line in your head.

2 ◁ Now align the clubface square to the target line by identifying an intermediate target just in front of you, such as an old divot mark or a leaf. It is easier to aim the clubface at a close target than at an object some 200 yards distant.

3 ◁ Secure your hands comfortably on the grip and then build your stance around the clubface. Remember the tips on achieving good posture discussed in Chapter 4 and keep your knees flexed while bending forward from the hips. Try to get everything as square to the bottom edge of the clubhead as possible; in other words, in perfect parallel alignment. Remember, your body alignment determines the path along which the clubhead is swung, and is crucial to a good shot.

4 △ Once you're set, waggle the clubhead back and forth a couple of times to ease the tension in your hands, arms and shoulders. This relaxation promotes fluidity of movement. Provided your posture is also good, you are now in great shape to swing the club correctly away from the ball.

● The swing itself is, to a large degree, a chain reaction. One good move generally leads to another. Make a mistake, though, and yes, you've guessed it, another mistake usually follows. That's why the first move away from the ball is so critical - it sets the pattern for your entire swing.

THE BACKSWING
THE FIRST LINK IN THE CHAIN

2 ◁ This movement is referred to in golfing language as the one-piece takeaway, and it is by far the most reliable method. The clubhead moves away low to the ground, gradually arcing inside the target line as the body rotates and the left arm extends away.

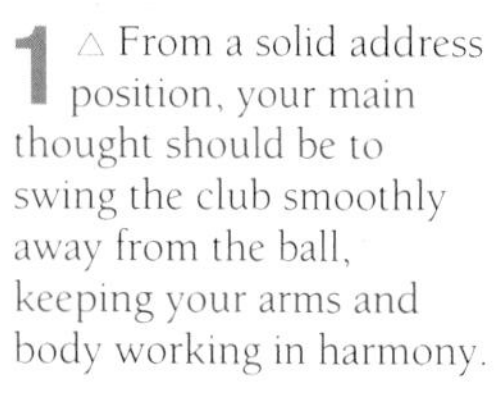

1 △ From a solid address position, your main thought should be to swing the club smoothly away from the ball, keeping your arms and body working in harmony.

3 ◁ Naturally the wrists should hinge (or 'set') in harmony with the swinging motion of the clubhead. Keep in mind that as the arms swing, so the body rotates. Each component part works together - your arms should never work independently of the rest of your body.

4 ▷ As you reach the top of the backswing, your club should still be on line, parallel to the target.

5 △ There are two possible errors in club alignment that are sometimes introduced at the top of the swing. Firstly, you can find yourself in a laid-off position, where the club points left of target.

6 △ The opposite to this is when your club is across the line, or pointing to the right of the target. Each of these positions is an indication that you have swung the club away from the ball incorrectly. As a result of this, you will probably deliver the clubhead to the ball incorrectly, causing a crooked shot.

● The downswing is a reaction, not an action. Everything that happens depends upon what has gone before, which is why your grip, your posture, your alignment and your backswing are so important. For every link in the chain that you perform correctly, the chances of getting everything right at impact increase. Remember that the downswing images that you see here are positions within one continuous motion. You swing **through** these positions, not **to** them.

THE DOWNSWING
HOW IT CLICKS INTO PLACE

1 ◁ The transition period from the end of the backswing to the start of the downswing is critical. Try to feel that you start your downswing with a subtle move of your left knee towards the target, combined with a gradual weight-shift on to your left foot. In modern 'golf-speak' this is referred to as leg separation.

2 △ The beauty of this move is that it initiates an unwinding of your hips and torso, which automatically slots your hands and arms down into an ideal position to attack the ball from the inside.

3 △ Now you're on track to deliver the club-head square to the back of the ball. Bang!

4 △ Through impact, your hands and arms free-wheel up and around into the perfect follow-through position, which is the mark of a good player.

5 ◁ By this stage, of course, it's far too late to influence the outcome of the shot. But it's a good idea to imagine yourself finishing in a balanced, poised position. It promotes an unhurried, controlled action and removes any tendencies to swing too hard.

● The shape of your swing is determined by a combination of your height, build and the length of your arms. Provided you correctly coordinate the turning motion of your upper body and the swinging motion of your arms, the swing plane will take care of itself.

SWING PLANE AND TEMPO

How fast or slow you swing the club again depends entirely on the individual. Lanny Wadkins swings at a very brisk tempo, but the important point is that his rhythm remains constant from start to finish. On the other hand, someone like Ben Crenshaw swings relatively slowly. The one thing that separates tour pros from the handicap golfer is the ability to maintain a consistent rhythm. Fast or slow is irrelevant - the fact that it is in time is all that matters.

You too need to find your own best pace at which to swing the club - a tempo that allows you to stay in control of your movements.

Above: Brett Ogle tends to adopt an upright shape.
Left: Ian Woosnam is renowned for having a relatively shallow, rounded swing.

'The one thing that separates tour pros from handicap golfers is the ability to maintain a consistent rhythm'

1 ◁ Naturally, how far you stand from the ball has an effect on your swing plane. A long club such as a driver will cause you to stand further from the ball.

2 ◁ This will cause you to have a fairly flat, shallow swing plane.

1 ◁ On the other hand, the 9-iron has a much shorter shaft which requires you to stand closer to the ball.

2 ◁ From such a position, your swing will automatically become steeper and more upright.

● Hitting the ball long distances is a product of good technique - it's your reward, if you like, for paying attention to the fundamentals of the swing. As the legendary teacher John Jacobs has often said: 'Distance is achieved through clubhead speed correctly applied'. This exercise can help you accentuate some of the key factors which cause the ball to fly further.

ACHIEVING MAXIMUM DISTANCE

1 ◁ One of the most common errors that cause loss of distance is when you chop down on the ball much too steeply.

2 ▽ To prevent or cure this fault, you should practise hitting drives from an extra high tee-peg. Set up using your normal routine.

3 △ Make sure that you keep the clubhead hovering off the ground. If you were to chop down too steeply on a ball teed *this* high, you'd miss it altogether.

4 ◁ The extra height encourages you to sweep the clubhead away from the ball on a shallow arc, encouraging you to make a more rounded, less up-and-down swing.

5 ◁ Not only does this exercise help you to coil more effectively in the backswing, it also stops you from becoming too steep in the downswing and encourages you to sweep the ball away.

6 △ Practise this technique and you'll strike the ball more solidly, which will have the desired result of making it travel further.

CHAPTER 8

Bobby Jones once said that 'the difference between a sand trap and a water hazard is the difference between a car crash and a plane crash. You at least have a chance of recovering from a car crash'. Ernie Els, like most top-class golfers, usually capitalises on this opportunity to recover.

Sadly, most club golfers see it differently. Bunker play remains something of an unknown quantity and indeed for some, recovery is out of the question. That's something you have to change. Bad bunker play can breed negative thinking throughout your game. Armed with the right technique, though, you can remove sand-phobia and look forward to more professional results, all crafted by your own hand. Now doesn't that sound good.

BUNKER PLAY

● One of the keys to becoming a better bunker player is understanding that the bounce effect created by the specially designed sole on the sand wedge is best utilised when the clubface is open, i.e. aligned to the right of your target. So your set-up is crucial.

MASTER THE **REGULAR SPLASH SHOT**

1 △ You need to open your stance by aligning your body, especially your hips, shoulders and feet, to the left of the target. Shuffle your feet down into the sand to provide a secure footing and adopt a slightly wider stance than normal - try to feel settled over the ball. Now take your grip, but make sure that the clubface is open in relation to your stance and is pointing a little to the right of the target.

2 △ Now, take the club back initially along the line of your feet, keeping the open alignment of the clubface.

3 △ As the club swings back, hinge your wrists to set it on a slightly steeper plane. You must ensure that the clubface stays open through impact. If you allow the clubface to close, the ball will fly to the left and too far.

5 ◁ The open clubface combined with an out-to-in swing path sends the ball floating straight towards the flag. That's what good bunker play is all about - having the confidence to splash the clubhead into the sand at the correct angle of descent, trusting the design of the club to do the rest for you.

6 ◁ As a useful guide to the length and force of the swing required, imagine you are playing a shot from the fairway twice as long as the one facing you in the sand. So for a 30-foot bunker shot, you need the force of a 60-foot pitch. This will compensate for the cushioning effect of the sand at impact.

4 △ In the downswing, you need to smoothly accelerate the clubhead through the sand under the ball. This creates a splash effect, although you don't need to remove great quantities of sand.

● This is the one situation where you can throw away the normal bunker shot textbook. Playing from a plugged, or buried, lie calls for changes to your club, your address position and your swing.

EXPLODE FROM **THE BURIED LIE**

1 △ When the ball is buried, you need to use your pitching-wedge, not your sand-wedge. The design of the sand-wedge encourages the clubhead to slide through sand, and in this case that's not ideal. Here you need the clubhead to dig down into the sand underneath the ball, and the relatively sharp leading edge of your pitching-wedge is better suited to that task.

2 △ You do not open the clubface at address and neither do you open your stance. Instead, you should stand square to the target, with the clubface square and with the ball back in your stance, towards the right foot.

3 △ With all the elements of a good set-up in place, you need to commit yourself to being fairly aggressive with this shot. On the backswing, pick the clubhead up a little steeper than you would for a normal bunker shot.

'With lots of application, and a little bit of luck, you'll hit your fair share of these shots pretty close to the hole'

4 △ You need to concentrate on striking down into the sand behind the ball. Ensure that your left wrist stays rock-solid through impact, and don't be afraid to hit down hard.

5 △ A lot of sand will be lifted up, so you need to generate a great deal of forward momentum in order for the ball to clear the front lip of the bunker.

6 △ The ball is bound to come out low and it's impossible to generate backspin, so allow for plenty of run from a plugged lie.

● The fairway bunker shot, where you're having to cover a long distance, is unlike any other shot from sand. In many ways it is just like playing a shot from the fairway, only there is even greater emphasis on the necessity to strike the ball cleanly. You simply cannot afford to let sand come between the clubface and the ball.

THE FAIRWAY BUNKER
MAXIMISING THE DISTANCE

1 △ Your first priority is clearing the front lip of the bunker. Once you have chosen the correct club to do this, then you can assess whether or not you can reach the target. If you can't, then don't be tempted to try a longer club - just settle for progressing the ball well down the fairway. Take your chosen club and slide (or 'choke') down on the grip an inch or two. This increases the likelihood of perfect contact, while having the added benefit of shortening your swing and enhancing your control.

2 △ With the ball positioned in the centre of your stance, commit yourself to making a controlled, three-quarter swing from a solid stance.

3 △ If your feet are settled securely down into the sand, this will naturally 'quieten down' your leg action and help make your swing tidy and compact.

4 ◁ If you've chosen your club wisely, and executed the shot in a controlled fashion, you'll clip the ball cleanly, with the merest puff of sand through impact.

5 △ You're back on the move again, having negotiated a hazardous bunker without falling behind in your score.

● Like anything in golf, good bunker play comes through a knowledge of the correct techniques and a commitment to practise what you learn. Here are some ideas for you to work on in your sand play.

PRACTISE IN THE SAND

2 ◁ Now play each shot. Splash the clubhead down into the sand on the first line and imagine the clubhead coming out of the sand on the exact spot where you drew the second line. This helps remove the tendency to dig too deep and also encourages you to swing through the sand under the ball.

BETWEEN THE LINES

1 △ This exercise will help you visualise the correct contact you need to make in the sand. Line up three or four balls in a row and draw two lines either side - one a couple of inches in front of the balls and another the same distance behind them.

3 ◁ You might even try this action without the ball, just to get used to the feel of splashing the clubhead through the sand. Once you're familiar with that sensation, play shots for real and simply let the ball get in the way of your swing.

THE UPHILL EXPLOSION SHOT

1 △ The key factor when playing from any kind of slope is to manufacture your set-up in such a way that you can make as normal a swing as possible. In sand, the same principle applies. Lodge your feet into the sand as high up the slope as you can comfortably manage, with your weight settled back over your right knee. Ideally, your shoulders should now be at the same angle as the slope and the ball opposite the inside of your left heel.

2 ▷ Now focus on a spot roughly two inches behind the ball and commit yourself to splashing the clubhead down into the sand on that exact spot. Keep your weight back on your right side and make sure that the clubhead swings up the slope, through the sand and out.

3 △ Don't lean into the slope - you'll only succeed in burying the clubhead so deep into the sand that the ball travels no distance at all. The combination of the upslope, your altered set-up and the shape of your swing ensures that the ball pops up high into the air and stops on landing almost immediately. So don't worry too much about over-shooting the target. Try and land the ball on top of the flag-stick, which will help prevent you from leaving the ball well short.

COMMON COMPLAINT

A big mistake many golfers make is in assuming that brute force is required to dislodge a ball from the sand. They attempt to blast the ball out in a great spray of sand, with disastrous results. This is the kind of approach that leads to total misery.

DON'T DIG TOO DEEP

1 ◁ With no real grasp of the correct technique you try to hit the ball too hard, which causes you to fall back on to your right foot. From here you either 'thin' the ball or punch into the sand and catch it heavy.

2 ▷ The end result is usually the same however you make contact. The ball remains in the sand, causing you to drop a shot and creating feelings of anger and frustration. A vicious circle often develops, with you trying to hit the ball even harder at the next attempt.

CLASSIC CURE

Providing the lie is good, there is absolutely no need to employ muscle tactics to escape from a bunker. You need to try and visualise the clubhead travelling on a U-shape path into and through impact. See if this helps.

THINK OF A 'U' SHAPE

1 △ Take the club back, as in the classic bunker swing, hinging your wrists to set the club on a slightly steeper backswing plane.

2 △ From here, start the downswing by shallowing the angle of the shaft, which causes the club to move into a slightly more horizontal position.

3 △ You can now swing the clubhead down and through the sand on a much shallower angle of attack, thus achieving more consistent contact.

4 ◁ There's no more digging deep into the bunker. Instead, the clubhead splashes in and out of the sand, which has a kind of cushioning effect, throwing the ball out on a high-flying, soft-landing trajectory.

CHAPTER 9

Learning to manoeuvre the ball through the air in different ways is definitely advanced technique. But it isn't rocket science. Seve Ballesteros is the ultimate master craftsman - if there's a gap in the trees, you can be sure he'll find it - but all good players have the ability to shape their shots at will.

There are two main contributing factors which dictate the flight of the ball; the alignment of the clubface at impact, and the path of the swing into and through impact. Getting them right is the key to good golf. The techniques shown in this chapter will help you understand and use these factors to best advantage, and give you a valuable aid to escaping from trouble or improving your strategy. Not only will this knowledge help you manufacture shots intentionally, but it will also enable you to pinpoint your faults simply by looking at the flight of the ball as it curves through the air.

SHAPE YOUR SHOTS

● A draw shot (sometimes known as the hook) is when you impart sufficient spin to the ball for it to swing to the left once it is in the air. Shown here is an ideal situation in which to play the draw. With water on the left of the fairway, you can aim down the right and let the ball drift back towards the middle. Even if the draw doesn't materialise, the worst that can happen is that you'll end up in the light rough on the right.

THE DRAW SHOT

1 △ Aim the clubface at the target, then align your feet, hips and shoulders slightly to the right of that. How far right you aim depends on how much draw-spin you require. Note that the spin makes the ball run a lot further than normal, so allow for this when you consider such factors as club selection and a landing area.

2 ▷ You need to 'strengthen' your left-hand grip just a fraction, i.e. by twisting it clockwise slightly so three or three-and-a-half knuckles are showing from the front rather than the normal two.

3 ▷ In the backswing, concentrate on making a good turn, swinging in a rounded action as opposed to keeping a straight back.

4 ◁ At the top of the backswing the shaft of the club should point to the right of the target. How far right depends on how far you intend to shape the ball.

5 ▷ As you swing down, attack the ball from 'inside' the line, sweeping the club across the target line from left to right. The clubface isn't closed to the target - it's aiming straight at it - but in relation to your stance and the path of your swing it is closed. It is this that imparts the necessary sidespin to the ball to make it move from right to left through the air. It will take off to the right of the target line, then gradually curve back in to the left.

● The fade, or slice in its extreme form, is the opposite of the draw and hook. Therefore, you need to recreate the exact opposite impact factors in order to make the ball spin the other way. Here, a tree is blocking a direct path to the hole - and it's too close to fire straight over it. A low, cutting fade is the best shot for the job.

THE LOW FADE

1 △ Aim the clubface at the target, but this time align your hips, feet and shoulders to the left of the line. This encourages you to swing very slightly from out-to-in, which helps impart the necessary side-spin.

2 ▷ Choke down on the grip an inch or two and also weaken your left-hand hold by moving it slightly clockwise. This helps ensure that the clubface does not close to the left at impact.

3 △ Now swing back along the line of your feet for the first 18 inches of the takeaway. Try to make your swing a little more upright than normal.

4 △ At the top of the backswing, the shaft of the club should point to the left of the target. You can ask a friend to study this for you, or else practise it at home while standing in front of a mirror.

5 △ In the downswing the clubhead approaches the ball from outside the target line. Again, geometry does the hard work for you. Through impact, try to sense that the back of your left hand faces the target for just a fraction longer than normal. This ensures that you maintain the necessary clubface angle to create sidespin on the ball.

6 △ Note how the follow-through is a little 'held-off'. For this type of shot that's a very positive sign. The angles you create at address ensure that the clubhead travels slightly across the line, or out-to-in, through impact. And as the clubface is open in relation to the path of your swing, you automatically create the necessary sidespin to produce a shot that starts to the left then fades to the right through the air.

● Here, the same tree is blocking a path towards the hole. If you don't fancy your chances of playing the big left-to-right shot, there's always another option - fly straight over it. Risky? No, not really, providing you have a good understanding of the necessary techniques.

THE HIGH SHOT OVER THE TOP

1 △ As we've already shown, working the ball different ways through the air is a game of opposites. When you need to hoist the ball high into the air, you should merely think of adopting the opposite techniques from those that are required to hit the ball low.

2 ◁ If you were about to kick a football as high as you possibly could, you'd lean back, wouldn't you? You need to do a similar thing here. Settle more of your weight on the right side than on the left; a ratio of roughly 60/40 is perfect. The ball should be two or three inches further forward in your stance. This helps position your upper body in behind the ball and automatically places your hands directly above the clubhead, which will cause a little more loft than on a conventional shot.

3 ▷ Swing the club back a little more steeply than normal to try and encourage the necessary steep angle of attack in the downswing.

4 ◁ Above all, try to stay behind the ball as much as possible through the hitting area.

5 ▷ Keep your head hanging back behind the point of impact, until the momentum of your arms and the clubhead pull you through.

6 ◁ All you then need to do is finish high, in perfect balance, and watch the ball soar over the tree-top.

● This shot is potentially your best weapon in strong wind. If you have the ability to keep the ball low when the wind is up, you're at a massive advantage over anyone who cannot. And besides, there will be plenty of occasions when overhanging branches force you to hit the ball low. So, it pays to know how.

SHOOTING LOW BEATING THE WIND

1 △ The last thing you need in a head-wind, of course, is loft. So take a slightly longer club than otherwise and place the ball back in your stance, roughly two to three inches nearer your right toe than normal. Then gently press your hands forward of the clubhead so that your left arm and the shaft form a straight line down to the ball. In a very strong wind you should also experiment with a wider stance than normal to help you keep your balance. When you set the ball back in your stance a common mistake is to aim the clubface out to the right, so make sure you are still aiming at the target.

2 △ There is an old golfing adage, 'Into the breeze swing with ease'. The one thing you must resist at all costs is the urge to hit the ball harder. It generates more backspin and that immediately causes the ball to fly high. Into wind, that's disastrous. So make a conscious effort to swing even more smoothly than normal. You're gripping down on the club, so that helps reduce your swing to three-quarter length. The swing is also more of an arms-and-shoulders controlled action with wrist-break kept to a minimum.

3 △ Keep your weight central and over the ball as you begin the downswing.

4 △ As you reach impact, try to keep the clubhead low to the ground into and through the ball. This helps to ensure that you do not swing too steep, which again, is one of the factors that creates height.

5 ◁ The follow-through is no more than three-quarter length, either, which is a sign that you're swinging easier to achieve the same result. That's smart wind play.

'Into the breeze swing with ease'

● The key to playing a good shot from an uphill or downhill lie is in altering your set-up in such a way that you can swing as normally as possible. Here's a demonstration of that theory.

SLOPING LIES

THE UPHILL LIE

First, let's take a look at the uphill lie. Straight away you should recognise that the upslope will make the ball fly much higher than normal, so take a longer club than you would on a flat lie from the same distance. Not only will the ball fly high, you'll also have a tendency to pull the shot left, so allow for this when you aim.

1 △ At address, position the ball a fraction further forward and try to set your shoulders on a fairly level plane with the slope of the fairway. You'll see that your head is now well behind the ball and you should endeavour to maintain that relationship at least until impact. In effect, your stance is now as normal as it can possibly be - you've built your position around the slope.

2 ◁ Transferring your weight in the backswing shouldn't be a problem - the slope is helping you in that regard - so make sure that at the top of the backswing your weight is supported over a flexed right knee.

3 △ In the downswing, just concentrate on swinging the clubhead along the contours of the slope, through impact, to a balanced finish.

THE DOWNHILL LIE

From the downhill lie, you need to use a shorter club than usual to gain any loft on your shot. Again the key is to build your stance around the slope.

2 ▷Your key thought in the backswing should be on making a good turn. The downslope will naturally keep your weight more centred over the ball. You just need to make sure your weight doesn't shift further down the slope.

1 △ With the ball back in your stance, set your shoulders as level to the slope as you can comfortably manage . You should also keep your weight over the left side ever so slightly - a ratio of 60/40 is ideal.

3 ◁ In the downswing you must resist the tendency to help the ball into the air - that will only lead to a poor strike. Accept the fact that the ball will fly lower than normal and commit yourself to swinging the clubhead as far down the slope as possible - almost as if you're chasing after the ball as it flies.

● Once you have an understanding of the techniques required to shape your shots, the key is to cultivate that ability to such an extent that your are confident enough to play the shots during a proper round.

VARY YOUR PRACTICE

Next time you're on the practice ground, select a mid-iron and 'call the shots' to yourself. Hit a fade with one ball and a draw with the next. Then a high shot followed by a low shot.

Vary your shots, but not your target area. You want to learn how to get from A to B in as many different ways as possible - you never know when a huge tree might force you to take an unconventional route. This also helps you develop an awareness of the position of the clubhead throughout the swing - and that's very good for your golf.

Sloping lies affect the flight of the ball through the air, so it's important you practise from these situations, too.

'Vary your shots but not your target area'

1 △ With the ball below the level of your feet, you are forced to bend over a little more from the hips.

2 △ This alters your spine angle and leads to a more upright swing plane. That tends to result in a shot that fades to the right.

3 △ Conversely, when the ball is above your feet it is necessary to stand a little more upright.

4 △ This leads to a more rounded swing plane, which tends to cause you to draw the ball. If you can learn to allow for these deviations, you are better equipped to handle sloping lies on the course.

CHAPTER 10

GOLF'S SIX DEADLY SINS

It's true to say that the player who usually wins is the player who makes the fewest mistakes. Never was there a better example of this than Nick Faldo's first Open Championship victory at Muirfield in 1987. In the final round, he made 18 consecutive pars - no birdies, but more significantly, no bogeys. Meanwhile, his closest challengers crumbled around him.

But it's not just making the fewest mistakes that counts, winning is also about avoiding the really serious howlers. Those killer shots that cause double and treble bogeys, the bane of every mid- to high-handicapper's life. The slice, the shank, the top - you know the ones. The key to eradicating these shots, of course, is to know exactly how they happen. So in this chapter we explain, and cure, the six deadliest sins in golf.

1 DEADLY SIN THE PERSISTENT SLICE

This, without any shadow of a doubt, is golf's public enemy number one. The slice, where the ball curves severely from left-to-right through the air, is an infuriating shot, made worse by most golfers' apparent inability to do a single thing about it. It's caused by a combination of an out-to-in swing path and an open clubface. The degree to which you slice the ball is totally dictated by these two factors.

CURE TRAIN AN INSIDE ATTACK

If you remind yourself of the two factors that cause a slice, namely an out-to-in swing path and an open clubface, it is easy to identify the ideal cure. You need to swing the club from the inside - or to be more precise, from inside to square to inside - and square up the clubface at impact. Simple, really. But we all know that actually putting the theory into practice isn't so easy. See if this exercise can bring about a change in fortunes.

1 △ Take your driver or 3-wood and address the ball, this time dragging your right foot back from your left.

2 △ This address position results in a dramatic change in the shape of your swing. For one thing, it encourages a better turn away from the ball.

1 △ Here we see a typical slicer's action. Even from a reasonable position at the top of the backswing, the shot is destined for failure as soon as the shoulders and arms throw the clubhead outside the line.

2 △ From there, the clubhead chops across the line on an out-to-in path, causing the ball to start left and swerve viciously in the air. A poor hand action and open clubface just make things worse.

3 △ More significantly, it helps prevent your upper body throwing the clubhead outside the line from the top. Instead, your arms swing the club down from inside the ball-to-target line.

4 △ Your hands and arms start to work more effectively, delivering the clubface to the ball and through impact on the correct path. Suddenly, your shots don't start left and slice. They start right and draw, a new phenomenon. Integrate this exercise into your practice routine so that you rehearse it, say, every other shot. You'll be amazed at the long term effect this will have on your swing and the quality of your shots.

2 DEADLY SIN
TOO MANY SKIED DRIVES

The skied drive - where the clubhead chops down, striking the bottom half of the ball and sending it virtually straight up in the air - can be caused by a number of faults. Contrary to popular belief, it is not necessarily the result of teeing the ball too high, although that's something you should nonetheless check.

CURE WORK ON A FLATTER PLANE

The driver, more than any other club in your bag, needs to be swung such that you sweep the ball away. So, to set about eliminating the sky and making sure you hit the ball solidly, you need to shallow your downswing attack.

1 △ Try this exercise. Address the ball as you would normally and then raise the clubhead 12-18 inches off the ground.

2 △ Now, try to swing the club away on a more rounded plane. Concentrate on synchronising your arm-swing with your upper-body turn.

1 ◁ More than likely, your posture is poor, inhibiting your turn and causing you to swing the clubhead up and down too steeply.

2 ◁Sometimes it is simply a case of trying to hit the ball too hard from the top. Whatever the cause, the end product isn't too pleasing.

3 ▽ Unwind your upper body and swing your arms on a similarly rounded plane, all the way through to the finish.

4 △ Rehearse this several times, back and through, back and through, to familiarise yourself with the sensation of turning and swinging on a flatter plane. When you're comfortable with this movement, hit shots for real. If you persevere, your downswing attack should gradually become shallower and you'll find that your shots start to go forward more than they go upward.

3 DEADLY SIN
HURT BY A VIOLENT HOOK

A hook is the opposite of a slice. And while it isn't quite as common a fault, it is no less destructive and equally difficult to shake off. It's basically the result of the clubhead approaching the ball from way inside the target line. Coupled with a closed clubface this causes the ball to start right and bend severely to the left.

CURE GET YOUR SWING BACK ON TRACK

Remember how we set about curing the slice? Well, to cure the hook we're going to do the opposite exercise by twisting slightly to the left.

1 ◁ Address the ball as normal, only this time drag your left foot back so that the toe is level with your right heel. As you do this, it's very important to try and keep your shoulder-line parallel to the target. Take a close look at your grip. Make sure you place your hands in a neutral position on the grip at address. Remember the quick check from Chapter Four – the Vs formed by the thumb and forefinger on each hand should point up towards your right eye.

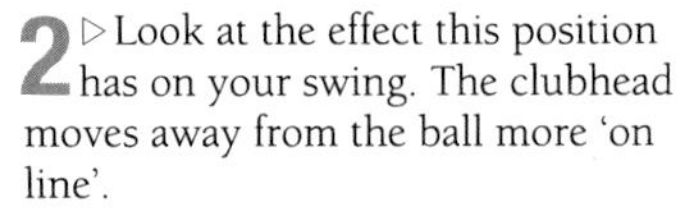

2 ▷ Look at the effect this position has on your swing. The clubhead moves away from the ball more 'on line'.

1 ◁ This is where the problems start. See how the club is taken back way on the inside with the clubface 'hooded' - in other words, looking at the ground. The shoulders are over-dominant and there's not nearly enough arm-swing. When you're this far on the inside at such an early stage, it becomes very difficult to recover. More than likely you'll either over-compensate by throwing the clubhead outside the line from the top, or, as in this case, continuing to swing on a severe in-to-out path. Coupled with a closed clubface, that's where your hook comes from.

3 △ Your arm-swing is more in tune with your body rotation, which also results in a better position at the top of the backswing.

4 △ Instead of hitting the ball from way inside the line, which is what causes the hook, you'll start to train a more on-line downswing attack.

5 △ Having your left foot drawn back also forces you to clear your left side in the downswing through impact - another factor which helps eliminate that damaging hook.

4 DEADLY SIN
FLUFFED CHIP SHOTS

Here's an embarrassing one. You're just off the green with only a short distance between you and the flag, in no obvious difficulty - but you fluff your chip shot three feet. Not only embarrassing, but very costly and intensely frustrating as well. So how is it possible to make such a hash of a relatively easy shot? And how can you prevent it happening?

CURE THINK 'ARMS AND SHOULDERS'

First, before we even move on to the techniques involved, bear this one thing in mind: always let the loft of the club do the work for you.

1 △ Now, the shot itself. Again, a useful maxim to work on at address is, 'hands forward, weight forward and ball back'.

2 △ Once you set up in that fashion, concentrate on making more of an arms-and-shoulders swing, allowing your body to rotate in time with the swinging motion of your arms.

3 △ Make sure that your wrists hinge only very slightly on the way back.

1 ◁ What usually happens is that you hinge your wrists too acutely in the backswing which sets you on far too steep an angle of attack. Now, with the clubhead travelling down so steeply it is impossible to achieve consistently good contact.

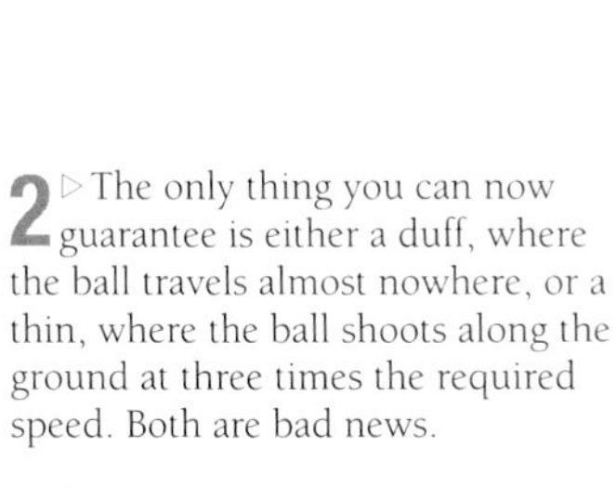

2 ▷ The only thing you can now guarantee is either a duff, where the ball travels almost nowhere, or a thin, where the ball shoots along the ground at three times the required speed. Both are bad news.

4 ◁ Retaining the angle in your right wrist as you move, swing your arms and rotate your body in unison down and through impact.

5 △ All through the downswing your hands should lead the clubhead into the ball, thus creating the descending angle of attack that is so crucial to good chipping. This is why it is so important to let the loft of the club do the work for you. You strike down to create height - no conscious effort or manipulation is necessary to get the ball airborne.

DEADLY SIN
THE REVERSE PIVOT

This fault can cause complete and utter power failure in the swing. The reverse pivot occurs when your weight shifts in the opposite direction to that which it should during the swing.

CURE HOW TO FEEL GOOD WEIGHT TRANSFER

In order to hit a golf ball as far forward as you possibly can, you must learn to transfer your weight correctly. Try the following exercise.

1 △ Address the ball, standing with your feet close together.

2 △ Swing the club back as normal and don't be afraid of a slight lateral movement to the right - that is far better than a reverse pivot.

3 △ The key to the whole exercise is to trigger your downswing into action by stepping towards the target with your left foot.

1 ◁ As the hands and arms swing the club away from the ball, your weight transfers on to the left foot.

2 ▷ As a consequence of this, your weight then transfers away from the target and on to your right foot in the downswing. Nothing good can come of it, that's for sure. While this demonstration is an exaggerated example, the fact remains that even the slightest hint of a reverse pivot seriously hinders your ball-striking ability. If this looks or sounds familiar, then it's time to get your weight moving in the right direction.

4 △ Really make an aggressive step to the left and feel that your entire body weight shifts noticeably on to your front foot through the hitting area.

5 △ Look at the difference this makes to the follow-through. Perfectly balanced with the weight supported by the left foot. Take a look at the difference in your shots, too. You'll enjoy that.

6 DEADLY SIN
TOO MANY THREE-PUTTS?

Golfers' tales of woe often revolve around the number of short putts missed. Sadly, this disguises the real cause of three-putting; namely, an inability to get approach putts close enough to the hole. No facet of your game is as vulnerable to self-imposed pressure as your short game. And once the trouble starts, it can take a long time to cure.

CURE LEARN TO FIND YOUR RANGE

If you can learn to develop a better feel for distance, your three-putt ratio is guaranteed to drop dramatically. There's no short cut, though. You've just got to take time on the putting green - time to work on some of the exercises demonstrated here.

1 ▷ To improve your judgement of distance, go to one side of the putting green and putt balls to the fringe at the opposite end. Try to leave each ball as close to the fringe as possible, without actually touching it. This enables you to concentrate solely on the weight of each putt without your having to worry too much about the direction.

2 ▷ Now an example of the perfect way to conclude your practice session. Putting to random targets is an excellent exercise because it closely simulates an on-course situation.

Simply drop a dozen balls down in one spot and putt each one to a separate target - the first to 20 feet, the second to 30 feet and the third to 40 feet. Tee-pegs are ideal targets as you can move them around the green at will. Repeat this four times until you've putted a dozen balls to three separate targets.

All the time try as much as possible to vary the distance and the amount of break involved for each putt. This improves your ability to see a putt and produce the necessary stroke to match. That gives you the confidence and the ability to achieve the same thing when you really need it most - in a competitive situation.

1 ◁ As you are probably well aware, every time you leave yourself three and four foot putts, the pressure on you to hole out increases. Eventually, you start missing them and then your confidence takes a serious knock. The situation then snowballs and you find yourself missing even more putts.

CHAPTER 11

PERFECT PRACTICE MAKES PERFECT

Gary Player, one of only four golfers to win all of golf's major championships, once famously remarked that, 'the harder I practise the luckier I get'. The great man was, and still is, one of the most diligent workers the game has ever known. The benefits are evident for all to see.

Whether degree of luck is directly related to level of practice is highly debatable. One thing is certain, though. Constructive, intelligent practice is the only reliable way to generate a long-term improvement in your game. Practice isn't just about bashing away hundreds of balls at the range, though. If you want to achieve perfect, you need to practise perfect. That's why sensible drills and exercises are so invaluable. Not only do they speed up the learning process, they also relieve the sense of tedium that many golfers associate with practising.

● Repetition is the key to this exercise. Its whole purpose is to make you familiar with the business of holing out from short range so that the job becomes as routine as you can possibly make it. Obviously there is more pressure on the course, but this exercise at least helps prepare you for those pressures. In all cases practise your putting with the same type of ball as you would use on the course. This helps you become accustomed to the feel of one particular ball, which is crucial in the quest towards being able to judge consistently the distance of your putts.

TRAIN A BULLET-PROOF PUTTING STROKE

1 △ Lay out as many balls as you like in 'bicycle-spoke' fashion, starting from 12 inches and working out to a distance of no more than 5 feet . Now set yourself the target of holing every ball in succession, either by working away from the hole along one line at a time or by holing the four nearest balls, followed by the four second-nearest and so on. Whatever method you choose, keep to a consistent pattern.

For something a little bit different – but extremely effective, nonetheless – try practicing your putting with a sand-wedge.

1 Hold the wedge slightly high, with the clubhead hovering level with the ball's equator.

2 Now, concentrate on striking the ball on the up. That's the key - you strike the ball right on its equator to promote a smooth roll.

3 If the ball jumps at impact, you've made a bad stroke. As your confidence grows, revert to making the same stroke using your putter.

2 △ If you miss one, no matter what stage of the exercise you are at, then you must start all over again. Be strict with yourself, too. This exercise loses all purpose if you do not punish your misses. Believe me, when you get towards the end of this exercise having not missed a putt, you'll start to learn what pressure is all about. And the more you learn to cope with that feeling, the fewer putts you'll miss in a competitive round.

● Whilst on longer putts the putter-head naturally travels back inside the line, it's a different story from short range. Ideally, the putter-head should travel square-to-square; in other words, straight back and straight through, with the putter-face staying square to the target-line throughout. The following exercise is specifically designed to groove a square-to-square putting stroke.

DEVELOP A SQUARE **PUTTING STROKE**

1 △ Identify a straight putt and place two planks of wood on the ground in such a way that they form a channel towards the hole. Now place a ball in between the two planks and line up the putter-face squarely to the hole. There should be roughly a half-inch gap either side of the toe and heel of the putter.

2 △ Now hit putts making sure that neither the toe or heel of the putter touches the planks of wood - just swing it straight back and straight through.

3 △ Provided you align the putter-face correctly you cannot miss. You needn't use planks of wood, of course. The shafts of two golf clubs are equally effective, as are a couple of flag-sticks. If you can just spend a couple of hours a week working on this exercise, you will be amazed at the difference it makes to your holing out potential.

'Provided you align the putter-face correctly you cannot miss'

And here's another good putting drill for you to work on - ideally in front of a mirror at home.

1 △ Trap the shaft of a club underneath your arms, across your chest, and address the ball as normal.

2 △ As you putt, make sure the shaft remains firmly in place against your chest.

3 △ This will help you to maintain the necessary shoulders-and-arms triangle formation, which is essential to a solid, repeating putting stroke.

● We've already stressed several times the importance of the role of the upper body. It's the engine room of your swing, if you like, so you'd better make sure it's always firing on all cylinders. Here's an exercise to help you appreciate the feeling of correct body rotation. It's also a great way to loosen up prior to teeing off on the first hole.

TRAIN A BETTER **BODY ROTATION**

1 △ Hold a club at either end and run the shaft across your shoulders and behind your head.

2 △ Don't stand in a lazy fashion - try to assume as close to perfect posture as you can. This encourages the upper body to behave as it should in the swing itself.

3 △ Now, simply rotate your upper body to the right so that the shaft of the club points to the ground in front of you. Keep your knees flexed and try to feel that your upper body is rotating against the resistance of your lower half. This process, referred to as coil, is the single most effective way to store up power in your backswing.

4 △ Complete the exercise by rotating your body to the left, through the impact area and on to the finish position. Try and keep your shoulders turning on a relatively level plane, rather than dipping and rocking. Repeat this movement as often as you like - every 10 shots during a practice session isn't a bad idea - and really get used to the feeling of rotating your upper body back and through.

'Keep your shoulders turning on a relatively level plane'

● All good chippers have a razor-sharp ability to judge height and roll around the greens. It's a talent born out of an understanding of which club performs best in certain situations - coupled with a die-hard commitment to practising that art. It's important that you, too, develop your own repertoire of strokes around the green because one thing is guaranteed; you'll always find a use for them.

THE HEIGHT AND ROLL **LEARNING CURVE**

1 △ Find a green where the pin is cut well on to the putting surface, thus giving you lots of room to work with. Drop down a bucket of balls and line up every club from your 7-iron to your sand-wedge. Chip one ball at a time, one club at a time, towards the same hole. Register the vital statistics for each shot: the height and trajectory; where the ball lands, how much it spins and how far it rolls. Familiarise yourself with these characteristics until they become second nature to you.

When you are next faced with a shot from just off the green, run your 'chip data' through your mind. First identify an ideal landing area, preferably on the green, to ensure a nice, even first bounce. Next, bearing in mind the proposed landing spot, visualise the amount of roll required on the shot to sweep the ball up towards the hole-side. Finally, select the club that performs that function best of all. Now go ahead and execute the shot just as you see it in your mind's eye. You'll be surprised how often you turn visualisation into reality.

● Impact isn't something you swing to, it's something you swing through. Nonetheless, there are several very effective ways of improving your impact position and thus the quality of your ball-striking. One such method was made famous by the great Henry Cotton, three-times winner of the Open Championship. He used to advocate swinging to the inside of an old car tyre. You don't necessarily need an old tyre, although for these purposes it is probably the most suitable prop. A heavy bag of sand or an 'impact bag' as shown here, which is sold in some professional shops, is equally effective. Whatever prop you use, this exercise is time well spent.

BUILD A BETTER SWING

1 △ Set up as you would for a normal shot and substitute your ball for an impact bag.

2 ▷ Now go ahead and swing into it as hard as you like. The fact that there is no object ball involved means that you cannot become too ball-oriented, thus encouraging greater freedom of movement and a more free swing of the clubhead. It also strengthens your wrists and promotes the concept of hitting against a firm left side. On top of all that, it encourages you to transfer your weight on to the left foot in the downswing. All of these factors are conducive to better, crisper, ball striking.

The following exercise is very effective for building your swing and improving your balance.

1 △ Take two clubs of similar length, a couple of mid-irons are ideal, grip them in baseball fashion and assume good golfing posture.

2 △ Now swing them simultaneously back and forth, very slowly and very smoothly.

3 ▷Concentrate on making a good turn away from the ball and a free-flowing swing through impact to a balanced finish. Then hold it there for a few seconds - if you can maintain perfect balance with two clubs you should have no problem when you're swinging just one.

Not only is this a great swing-building drill, it's also a perfect first tee loosener which helps get your golfing muscles tuned in to the business of hitting a shot.

● Golf, to paraphrase an old soccer term, is a game of two sides. So it's vital that you train both the left and right sides of your body to behave correctly during the swing. There are various ways of doing this.

ONE-ARMED SWING DRILLS

1 △ Grip the hosel of any club with your right hand only.

3 △ Then really whip the club through the 'hitting zone'. Allow your body to respond to the motion of your arm and listen to the club as it wooshes through the air.

2 △ As you swish the grip-end back, make a good upper-body turn and feel your right arm fold as it should in the backswing.

4 ◁ This exercise enhances the feeling of you straightening your right arm in the downswing, or re-establishing your arc as it is known in golfing terms. It also encourages the correct release through impact, essential to good shot-making. As you become more familiar with this sensation, take the exercise a stage further and hit half-shots with your right hand only. Make sure you tee the ball up and remember to take hold towards the bottom of the grip, where your right hand usually rests.

Now for an exercise that gradually builds up your left-side strength.

1 △ Again take your 7-iron, but this time grip it with your left hand only, otherwise adopting normal good golfing posture. Tuck your right hand in your pocket to keep it out of the way.

2 △ Make a number of three-quarter swings, concentrating on maintaining a smooth, unhurried and even tempo.

3 △ Feel the weight of the clubhead at the end of the shaft and accelerate smoothly through impact. If your grip is sound, the correct forearm rotation and wrist hinge will develop naturally in the swing.

4 ▷ Note the emphasis on the word 'smoothly' throughout this drill. And rightly so. If you try to hit these shots too hard you'll more than likely bring excessive body movement into the swing, and that defeats the object of this exercise. Even worse, you might cause yourself an injury. So build up slowly and, if necessary, don't be afraid to start the exercise by hitting half shots. Alternatively, clip a tee-peg out of the ground until you feel the strength in your left arm is sufficient to start hitting the ball.

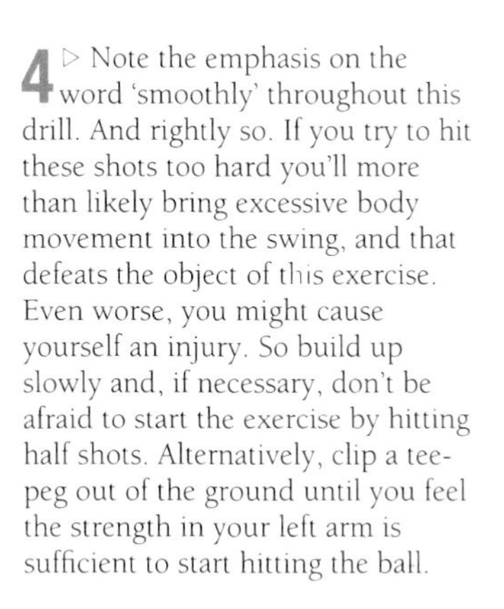

CHAPTER 12

SMART STRATEGY FOR LOWER SCORES

A smart strategy is the inconspicuous element of good golf. It doesn't manifest itself in spectacular fashion, like a towering long drive; nor does it turn heads and cause gasps, like a monster putt drained from 50 feet. But your strategic ability, or course management as it is often referred to, is at least as important as anything else you do in the space of 18 holes.

Tom Watson is recognised as one of the great thinkers of the game. His extraordinary record in the major championships is due in no small part to his immense powers of thinking and strategic shot-making. So if you want to shoot the best possible score you can, every time you tee up and irrespective of your form on the day, then it's time to get a smarter strategy.

● The first step towards improving your course management skills is to learn precisely how far you hit every club in your bag. OK, so you don't strike the ball with the same level of consistency as, say, Nick Faldo. But that shouldn't stop you from determining an average for each club. This at least enables you to make positive judgements out on the course, rather than your having to rely on guesswork and the vagaries of 'lady luck'.

KNOW YOUR DISTANCES

So, go to the practice ground with a full set of clubs and a bucket of balls. Now carry out the following exercise. Start with whichever club you feel happiest and proceed to hit 20 balls. Once you've done that, discard the longest five and the shortest five. Then pace out the yardage of the main cluster of balls to arrive at the average distance you hit that particular club. Write that information down on a note-pad and repeat the exercise with every club in your bag.

It takes time, but this exercise is worth every minute. Even if you play the same course week in week out - in fact, especially if you play the same course - knowing how far you hit each club gives you the confidence to swing freely. And that means more accurate iron shots.

● You've done all of your warm-up exercises and hit a few practice balls. Now it's crunch time - the first tee. Everyone gets nervous on the first tee at some stage. The professional feels nervous in the US Masters - you probably feel nervous in the annual Summer Meeting. There's nothing wrong with that, it merely shows that you are alert and ready to go. Here are a few rules you should stick to in order to help calm those butterflies in your stomach.

GETTING OFF TO A GOOD START

1 △ Go with a club you feel confident of hitting solidly and accurately. Don't feel that you have to reach for your driver, even if it's quite a lengthy hole. Use a lofted wood, or even a long iron if that's what you feel comfortable with. Distance really isn't that important. Getting the ball in play - on the short grass - is your first priority.

2 ▷ Take deep breaths prior to teeing up. There's nothing better for helping to calm yourself down. Also try jiggling your hands a little, as if you were shaking water from them, to help ease the tension.

3 △ Once you're ready, make a conscious effort to grip lightly, but securely. Your overriding thought should then be 'rhythm'. Everyone's natural tendency in a nervy situation is to get a little quick - you're not alone. So think about rhythm and simply swinging smoothly to a balanced finish. A good first tee shot is a real morale booster, so do all you can to get it right.

● The majority of club golfers pay very little attention to where they tee the ball. This is a wasted opportunity. There's more to teeing up than meets the eye and if you can learn how to best utilise every inch of the available teeing area, you'll make life a whole lot easier for yourself.

TEE UP INTELLIGENTLY

1 ◁ For example, let's say that, like most handicap golfers, your natural tendency is to hit the ball left-to-right - a fade on a good day and a slice on a bad one. In your case, then, you should tee your ball on the extreme right of the teeing ground and aim at the left side of the fairway. Look at the difference that makes to the size of your target area. You're aiming at the fat part of the fairway - that's particularly significant when there is trouble, such as a clutch of bunkers, on the right-hand side.

If you fade the ball, as planned, then your ball finishes in the middle of the fairway. Perfect. If you hit the shot dead-straight, you finish in the left half of the fairway or, at worst, the light rough. If your fade turns into a slice, then there's still a good chance that you'll find the fairway, or perhaps the light rough on the right. Your target area is increased enormously.

2 ◁ If, on the other hand, you tee your ball on the left side of the teeing ground, you get a very different perspective. The bunkers suddenly come more into play - it's very difficult to aim away from them, without aiming off the fairway.

Similarly, if your natural flight is a draw or hook, then you should tee up on the left of the teeing ground and aim down the right-hand side of the fairway.

1 ◁The same rules hold true on this par-3, played completely over water to a green that angles away from you. A tough one, no question. But if you tee up on the left side of the teeing ground, it becomes even harder. Even if you aim at the middle of the green, your margin for error is only small. And if you go for the pin, you're effectively giving yourself more water to fly over. That's the last thing you need.

2 ◁Look what happens when you tee up on the right side, though. From there you can aim more easily at the middle of the green, thus introducing a greater margin for error on either side. There's even a better angle to get at the pin, situated where it is on the back right edge. As you'll probably know all too well, on daunting holes such as this, every little bit helps.

Above: It's worth remembering the rule that allows you to tee the ball as much as two clublengths behind the teeing markers. If you're unsure of clubs on a par-3 hole, just moving back a fraction can make all the difference, and can actually help you make a more positive swing.

Left: If you want to shoot from the extreme left of the tee, you are perfectly entitled to stand outside the tee markers, providing your ball is teed within them.

● Think about the course you play most often and there are probably at least two or three holes that are usually out of reach in two shots. And if you're playing a monster of a course, then the number of three-shot holes is probably nearer half-a-dozen.

LAY-UP STRATEGY

1 Faced with a second shot on a hole that is just out of reach, most golfers pull out all the stops in order to get as close to the putting surface as is humanly possible. Not only is this risky - the harder you try to hit the ball, remember, the more you sacrifice accuracy - it is also an example of poor course management. If you hit the shot well, the chances are you'll leave yourself one of those tricky, fiddly, half-shots. And even the professionals try to avoid them.

2 A much more sensible strategy is to move up the fairway in two reasonable mid-distance shots, thus leaving you with a fairly full approach shot, ideally for a wedge or sand-wedge. This is even more important if the green is well guarded with bunkers at the front. These shots are much less likely to go horribly wrong, while they give you the ability to generate more backspin than with a short pitch. You now have the confidence to fly the shot over any trouble in front of the green, safe in the knowledge that the ball has sufficient backspin to sit down and stop fairly quickly.

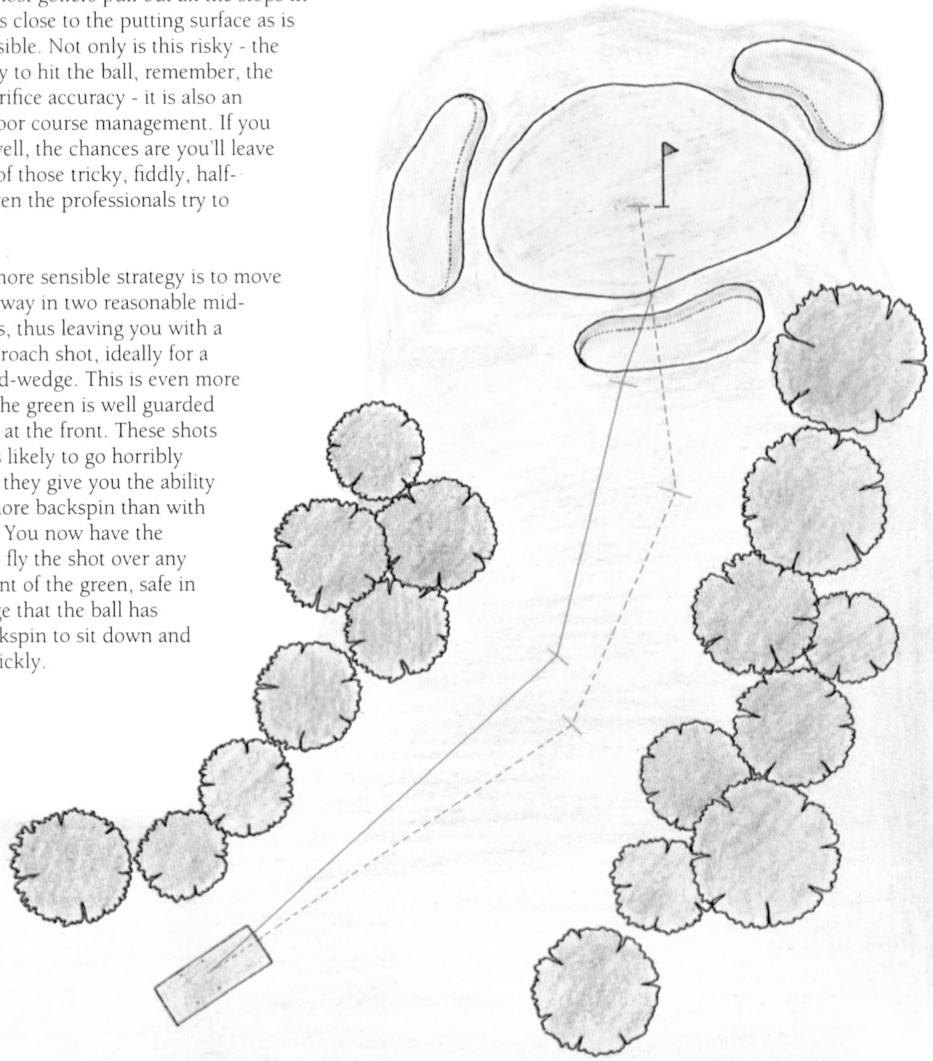

● It's always tempting to fire at the flag, irrespective of the length and difficulty of the shot, but it's not always the smartest strategy. Most greens are designed with more trouble on one side than the other. And on occasions where there's trouble on both sides, then usually either the back or front of the green is relatively safe.

GOOD APPROACH PLAY

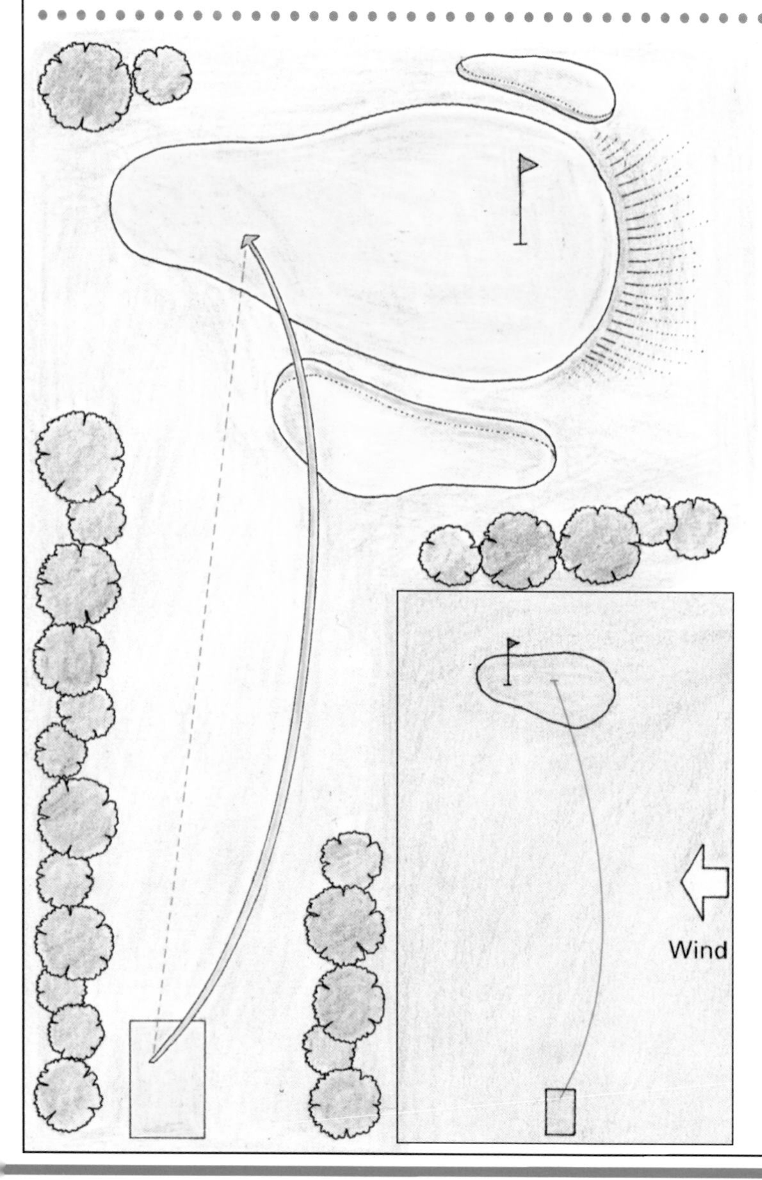

◁ When you draw up a game plan you need to identify where the safe side is on every hole on the course - in other words, the best place to miss the green. There's always one spot where it is really tough to get up and down in two. It might be a clutch of deep bunkers, or a steep bank. Whatever the trouble, it's not where you want to be. Even if the pin is cut on that side of the green, you simply shouldn't go for it. It's not worth the risk. In this situation, you still aim for the green, but you just need to be a little bit smart and favour the safe side. This strategy is known as 'managing your misses'. Even if the shot doesn't go precisely according to plan, you should still avert disaster and thus have a very good chance of holing with a chip and a single putt.

USE THE WIND DON'T FIGHT IT
Working the ball into the wind - for instance, hitting a fade into a right-to-left breeze - shows a good degree of shot-making ability, but it's a tough shot to play. Whenever possible, make the wind your friend, not your enemy. It's far easier to ride your ball on the wind. So, in a right-to-left breeze, aim right of your target, make a normal swing and let the elements drift the ball back on line. Likewise, in a left-to-right wind aim left and let the ball drift in the air. Bear in mind, though, that when your ball is travelling with the wind it flies further, and generally runs more on landing. So always allow for that in your club selection.

CHAPTER 13

Golf is the only truly self-governing sport. Admittedly, in the professional game there are often tournament officials on call, should the need arise. But it's a different story at club level. When you're out there competing in the monthly medal, for instance, there'll be no referee out there to adjudicate - it's up to you to know the rules. In this chapter, you'll find clarification of some of the more likely rules problems that you might encounter in the space of 18 holes. It is by no means intended to be a definitive guide to the Rules of Golf, but it will at least give you a decent grounding and also help you appreciate that the rules are not there solely to punish you. They can actually save you shots - and that's definitely worth knowing about.

GOLF RULES YOU SHOULD KNOW

● Earlier in this book we've covered the subject of where to tee off - namely, a rectangular area two club lengths in depth, defined by the outside limits of two tee markers. Remember also that you can actually stand outside the tee markers, providing your ball is teed within them. But what happens if you tee off from the wrong place?

TEEING OFF

PLAYING FROM THE WRONG GROUND

Most courses have three teeing grounds at each hole. The most distant one is used by men in formal competitions, the middle one by men in everyday play, and the closest by women. Some courses also have a fourth tee ground which is used during championship-level competitions. If you tee off from the wrong ground, or even from in front of the tee markers, the penalty varies depending upon the type of game you are playing.

In matchplay, where each hole you win gives you a point, your opponent has the right to ask you to play the shot again with no penalty. Whether he or she chooses to exert that right usually depends on the quality of your shot and the terrain in which it lands.

In strokeplay, where every stroke counts towards your final score, it is a different story. You are immediately penalised two strokes and must then replay the shot - now your third - off the tee. If you tee off from the wrong teeing ground, and then fail to correct your mistake, you are disqualified.

BALL FALLS OFF TEE

If your ball falls off the tee-peg mid-swing, or even if you nudge it off the tee-peg at address, there is no penalty. You simply re-tee and start again.

PLAYING OUT OF TURN

In matchplay, if you tee off when it is actually your opponent's turn to play, then he or she can ask you to replay the stroke. In strokeplay, the shot stands and there is no penalty, but if you want to stay friends with your fellow competitor then you shouldn't make a habit of it.

If you play in front of the tee markers, in matchplay you can be asked by your opponent to shoot again, while in strokeplay you incur a two-stroke penalty.

If your ball falls, or is nudged, off the tee as you address, you just need to set it up and try again, with no penalty.

'You can tee off up to two club lengths behind the markers'

Make sure you tee off from the correct place.

● An obstruction is an artificial object and can come in one of two contrasting forms, movable or immovable. Natural objects which can be easily moved are known as impediments, but natural objects such as trees or bushes are defined as hazards and must either be played around or a penalty is taken.

HOW TO DEAL WITH OBSTRUCTIONS

Movable artificial obstructions can be shifted out of the way.

MOVABLE OBSTRUCTIONS

Examples of movable obstructions are such things as a rake, cigarette butt or empty drinks can. If such an object is interfering with your play you can simply remove it, even if your ball is in a hazard. If the ball moves in the process, you simply replace the ball in its original position with no penalty.

IMMOVABLE OBSTRUCTIONS

An immovable obstruction is an artificial object which cannot be easily moved. Examples are an artificially surfaced path, a greenkeeper's tractor (if the greenkeeper isn't around to move it, that is!) or a metal pole supporting a tree. For you to obtain relief from such an object, though, the obstruction must interfere with either your stance or your swing. In this case you are entitled to a free drop. Note that on the putting green you are also able to claim relief if an immovable obstruction is in your line of play.

You can only claim relief from an immovable object if it hinders your stance or swing.

LOOSE IMPEDIMENTS

These are natural objects such as stones, worm casts, twigs and leaves. Provided the loose impediment is not 'fixed' or 'solidly embedded', or lying in a hazard, it can be moved. So, a worm slithering along the ground can be moved, but not if it is half-submerged and thus what you might call 'solidly embedded'. If an insect is resting, even crawling, on your ball, you are allowed to dispose of the offending creature. A banana skin, or any other fruit skin, is classified as a loose impediment and can be moved. A divot is a loose impediment when detached, but not when it is replaced. You can also move a stone embedded in the ground, but only if it can be moved with ease. Loose soil on the fairway cannot be moved - but can when it lies on the green. The same is true of sand dislodged from a bunker. Compacted soil in the form of say, aeration plugs, can be moved - and it doesn't matter whether you're on the fairway or the green. A fallen tree is also a loose impediment and can be moved, but not if it is attached to its trunk. And the rules do allow you to enlist the help of your playing partners.

THE FREE DROP

1 ◁ This is used when your stance or swing is hindered by an artificial immovable obstruction, such as a staked tree or a sprinkler head. You can also take a free drop if your ball lands in ground marked off as under repair, or if it comes down in casual lying water.

2 ◁ The procedure is quite straightforward. First mark the exact position of the ball. Then locate the nearest point of relief, in other words a position where the object ceases to obstruct either your stance or your swing. Place a tee-peg in the ground on that exact spot. Next, measure one club length from that point and again, place a tee-peg in the ground. These two tee-pegs represent the boundaries of your final 'drop zone'.

3 ◁ Now, stand upright facing the target, hold your arm out at shoulder height and drop the ball so that it first strikes the ground within the two tee-markers. The ball must come to rest no nearer the hole and neither must it roll more than two clublengths from the point where it first struck the ground. You can now play from this position with no penalty added to your score.

● A number of other considerations come into play when you approach the green. Chipping and putting is a difficult enough business without adding to your problems by incurring penalty strokes. So it's important that you learn what you can and cannot do on the green.

ON THE GREEN

THE FLAGSTICK

Most golfers are aware that you can have the flag attended on or off the green, and that if the ball then hits the flag you are penalised in both instances. And that you have the right to have the flag taken out before you play a shot, irrespective of whether your ball is on the putting surface or not. But few players know that if you are playing a chip shot to a highly elevated green, you are entitled to have the flag held up above the hole in order to give you a better view of the flag. It cannot be held to the side, though. It must be kept upright directly over the hole.

THE LINE OF YOUR PUTT

You can repair pitch marks on your line before you putt, but you cannot repair spike marks. However, you can (and should) repair both types of damage after you've putted out. You are also permitted to sweep away loose impediments such as leaves, twigs and sand, but only with your hand or a club. Don't use anything else such as a towel or your hat. One other thing, don't ever let your caddie or your partner touch the putting surface to indicate the line of a putt. That's an immediate penalty. By all means have it pointed out for you, though.

If you are chipping up to a high green, you can ask for the flag to be held high, directly above the hole.

MARKING YOUR BALL

1 ◁ Should you need to move your ball from another player's line of play, the rules for the amateur game allow you to mark your ball with almost anything. The best thing is to use a coin or a ball-marker. And while the rules also allow you to place your marker to the side of the ball, even in front of it, it's easier to put it just behind the ball.

2 △ On wet days, though, be careful not to tap your marker down with your putter, as the marker can easily stick to the sole of the club. And although there is no penalty if this happens - you simply locate the spot where you think the ball came to rest and replace the marker - it can be a fairly unsettling and embarrassing experience.

● Natural hazards include bunkers, water obstacles and trees and bushes. In general they should be played around, unless the ball is in an unplayable lie. Note that you are the sole judge of whether your ball is unplayable, and it is also up to you to decide whether to try and play on or accept a penalty.

DEALING WITH HAZARDS

WATER HAZARD

The normal water hazard is identified by yellow stakes or markers. You can do one of three things when your ball comes to rest in such an obstacle. Firstly, you can play the shot as it lies. Be careful not to ground your club in the hazard, though, as this causes a penalty. Secondly, you can identify the point where the ball entered the hazard, then walk back keeping that point and the hole in a straight line, dropping the ball on that line under a penalty of one stroke. Finally, you have the option of going back to the spot where you played your last shot, dropping the ball there at the cost of one stroke.

LATERAL WATER HAZARD

The lateral water hazard is a special case, and is identified by red stakes or markers. In this situation you have the same three options as in a water hazard, plus two extra choices. You can choose to penalty drop a ball outside the hazard within two club lengths of the point where the ball last crossed the margin of the water hazard (although no closer to the hole). You can alternatively drop a ball on the opposite edge of the water hazard, using a point on the bank at the same distance from the hole as a reference position.

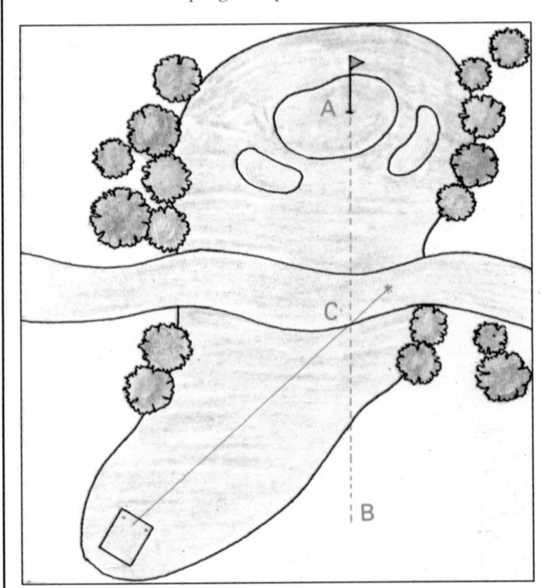

If your ball enters a water hazard, you can either play on, replay from where you made the shot, or else take a penalty drop. This must be on a line (A-B) which passes from the hole through the point (C) at which your ball crossed the edge of the hazard. You can drop on this line at any distance back from point C.

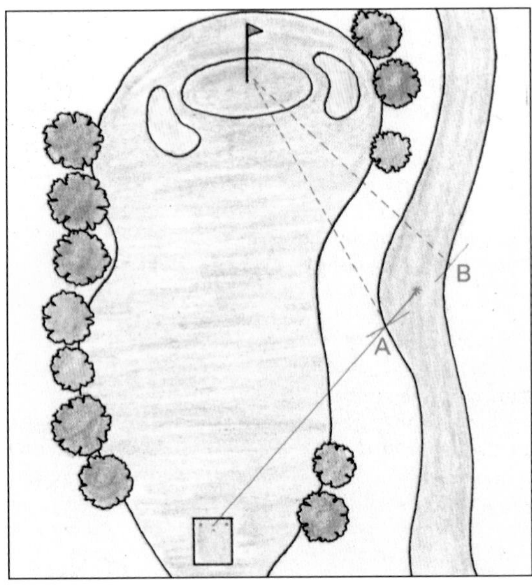

If the hazard is defined as a lateral hazard, you have a further two options to consider. You can make a penalty drop up to two club lengths from where your ball crossed the edge of the hazard (A), although you cannot move closer to the hole. Alternatively you can drop up to two club lengths from a point on the far edge of the hazard (B), which is at the same distance from the hole as point A.

THE BUNKER

1 △ The other common hazard is a bunker. The rules are plain and simple here - you don't touch the sand with the clubhead at address. So always hover the clubhead at a safe distance above the surface. This ensures that you don't touch the sand, and also gives you plenty of clearance in the early stages of the takeaway, when you can still be penalised for brushing the sand with the clubhead.

2 ▷ The only time the clubhead should come into contact with the sand is when you splash the ball out, high over the lip, hopefully in rather impressive fashion.

UNPLAYABLE LIE

If your shot has landed in an unplayable lie, for example, in the middle of a bush, you can be forced to take a penalty drop, where you add one stroke to your score for the hole before dropping the ball. You have three options here. Firstly, you can choose to go back and play a ball from a spot as near as possible to where you played your last shot. Secondly, you can make a drop within two clublengths' of the spot where your ball lies. (Note that you measure from where the ball lies, not from the nearest point of relief.) Thirdly, you have the option of making a drop behind where your ball lies, keeping that point directly between the hole and the spot on which the ball is dropped. There is no limit to how far back you can go.

IN THE ROUGH

Once you address the ball, which is defined as the moment you take your stance and ground the club, and the ball then moves, you receive a one-stroke penalty (unless you are on the tee). You then replace the ball back on its original spot and continue to play.

For this reason, when the ball is perched on long grass, or in any other situation where it might easily move, it is smart to hover the clubhead off the ground. If the ball moves, there is no penalty. Why? Because you haven't grounded your club and therefore cannot be said to have addressed the ball. You can now simply play the ball as it lies.

INDEX

ACKNOWLEDGEMENTS

The authors and publishers wish to thank the following people and organisations whose co-operation made this book possible: Mr Nagahara and the London Golf Club, Kent, England; Leigh Copolo from the London Golf Club; Nicola Way from Nizels Golf Club, Kent; Yonex and Maxfli.

Notes

Notes

Notes

Notes

Notes

Notes

Notes

Notes